ASSERTIVE WIZARD

HOW TO BOOST CONFIDENCE, GET YOUR MESSAGE ACROSS AND SPEAK WITH IMPACT

MARLENE GONZALEZ

LIFE COACHING GROUP LLC

Copyright 2021

All rights reserved. No part of this publication maybe reproduced, distributed, or transmitted in any form or by any means, including photocopying, recording, or other electronic or mechanical methods, without the prior written permission of the publishers, except in the case of brief quotations embodied in critical reviews and certain other noncommercial uses permitted by copyright law. For permission requests, contact the author through the website below:

www.marlenegonzalez.com

Hard Copy ISBN# 978-1-956253-02-3

Paperback ISBN # 1956253041

Audiobook ISBN # B09C6FJKZW

eBook ISBN # B099KNLYL1

CONTENTS

Join Our Community   vii
Introduction   xi

1. TAKE A STAND FOR YOURSELF   1
   What Is Assertiveness?   2
   Aggression vs. Assertiveness   3
   Benefits of Being Assertive   7
   Why Assertiveness Matters   9
   Tips for Practicing Assertiveness   10
   Why Self-confidence Matters   13
   Self-confidence vs. Self-esteem   14
   Benefits of Self-confidence   16
   Exercises for Building Self-confidence   20

2. EMOTIONAL INTELLIGENCE 101   25
   What Is Emotional Intelligence?   26
   Importance of Emotional Intelligence   28
   Do I Have High Emotional Intelligence?   29
   Measuring Emotional Intelligence   33
   Emotional Intelligence and Emotional Competence   37
   How to Communicate Your Emotions Effectively   40

3. GETTING THE MESSAGE ACROSS   46
   What Is Communication?   47
   Importance of Effective Communication Skills   48
   Benefits of Effective Communication   50
   Barriers to Effective Communication   52
   Guidelines for Effective Communication   54

Specific Guidelines for Business Communication	59
Specific Guidelines for Communication in Relationships	61
Models of Communication	64
Understanding Your Audience	67
4. PUT YOUR HEART AND PASSION INTO IT	**70**
The Can-do Attitude	70
How to Develop a Can-do Attitude	73
Developing Enthusiasm in Communication	77
How to Display Enthusiasm When Communicating	80
Reframing Your Problems	84
Importance of Reframing	85
How to Reframe Problems	87
5. SELF-MOTIVATION AND INSPIRING OTHERS	**91**
Self-motivation	91
Importance of Self-motivation	93
Self-motivation and Emotional Intelligence	95
How to Develop Motivation in the Workplace	97
Meditations for Boosting Motivation	105
How to Inspire Others	108
6. THE ART OF NEGOTIATING	**114**
How to Influence Others	115
Authenticity	117
Strategies for Professional Influence	117
How to Develop Negotiating Skills	124
How to Grow a Win-Win Mindset	130
7. SPEAKING WITH IMPACT	**135**

Conclusion	155
About the Author	169
Also by Marlene Gonzalez	171
References	173

This book is dedicated to every person of any race or age who dreams of unlocking the leader in them. The next generation of leaders: on your shoulders lays the responsibility to build a better world.

My husband, Carlos, thank you ,are my rock and thought partner. Thanks for your love and support. My sister, Vanessa, for her unconditional support in making my dream to write this series of coaching eBooks possible. My nieces and nephews (I would like to give you an additional edge as some of you are starting your professional journey).

This book is also dedicated to the Hispanic Alliance for Career Enhancement (HACE), a national non-profit dedicated to the employment, development, and advancement of Latino professionals. To all alumni, mentors, clients, and friends and family.

And finally to my publishing team (Nick, Myra, Kevin, Susan, Fahi and Dwinny and AIA Team and Publishing Life Services), you are awesome.

JOIN OUR COMMUNITY

Please, don't make the journey alone.

In order to maximize your investment in this book, I encourage you to join our support community on our website www.marlenegonzalez.com.

It is a support group where to share and learn leadership experience and valuable content. We often host free book/audiobook giveaways and helpful resources that will be key to your leadership journey.

It will be great to connect with you there,

Your coach, Marlene Gonzalez

"The basic difference between being assertive and being aggressive is how our words and behavior affect the rights and well-being of others."
– Sharon Anthony Bower

INTRODUCTION

In *The Wizard of Oz*, Dorothy encounters a character known as the Cowardly Lion. Though he is supposed to be a ferocious creature that dominates all other beasts, the Cowardly Lion doesn't seem to have any real courage. His attempts to scare Dorothy and her friends fail when she slaps him on the nose, leaving him crying uncontrollably. He confesses his cowardice and feels that he was born without any courage. Dorothy invites him to join them on their journey to see the Wizard who has the power to confer some courage upon the Cowardly Lion. After drinking a green liquid provided by the Wizard, the Cowardly Lion no longer feels afraid. He also receives a medal with the word *COURAGE* written across it.

But did the green liquid give magical courage to the lion? The truth is that the Wizard's gift was only a subconscious trigger that activated the courage *already* within the Cowardly Lion. It was his insecurities about not being like other lions that made him lose his assertiveness and confidence. Throughout their journey in Oz, the Cowardly Lion fought off beasts and saved his friends' lives many times. He had consistently shown his bravery despite being fearful, yet he was unaware of his innate courage. The Wizard's gift only helped him reframe his mindset to realize that courage is not the absence of fear. It is the confidence to step up in the face of adversity.

But what does this mean for you?

At every moment, you are presented with opportunities to express and assert yourself in your social interactions with others. Whether it's in an organization or your personal life, it is important to communicate confidently and speak clearly. Yet, being assertive and confident while communicating doesn't come easy for most people. Public speaking anxiety, also known as *glossophobia*, affects as much as 75% of the population. The research shows that more people are afraid of public speaking than they are of death! This is a startling statistic, and it goes to show just how deep-seated this fear is.

Maybe you are having trouble at work because you lack enough confidence to speak up for yourself. The office environment can be ultra-competitive, and it is often the case that those who can speak confidently and make an impact on others, especially their superiors, get more chances for upward mobility. If you lack the assertiveness necessary to be seen or heard, you may get passed up on promotions and end up feeling invisible to your superiors.

You could be one of those who has a problem saying "no" to other people. Your boss knows this, so they always pick you to stay late and work on some reports or saddle you with errands that aren't part of your job description. Maybe your colleagues ask you to cover for them or help them finish their work even as they leave the office early. Yet, you have never told them what you feel, and it's affecting your personal life as well. You are suffering in silence, despite knowing that being more assertive and confident can spare you the pain.

Maybe you are shy and public speaking isn't something that comes naturally to you. Yet, inside, you have this deep desire to learn how to express yourself more assertively in your relationships. It is said that effective communication is the bedrock of strong relationships. If you do not project confidence and personal power within your social circle, other people will inevitably dominate you in the relationship.

If you are romantically involved with someone but never get the courage to tell them what you want, they will assume all their decisions are fine with you. They may be making decisions that affect you negatively, but since you can't speak up, you always get the short end of the stick.

It is also possible that you struggle with speaking in front of a large or small audience. This may cost you many great opportunities to show others your capabilities. If you suffer from glossophobia, you are not alone. However, *you* want to overcome this fear, which is why you are reading this book. Being an effective communicator who confidently gets their message across will open up doors as more people become aware of who you are and what you can do. Someone in that group audience may connect you to a better career or a potential mate. You don't want to be the person who misses out on an awesome opportunity just because they couldn't speak effectively enough in front of people.

Conflicts are bound to arise whenever two or more individuals are unable to communicate well with each other. This can get worse when you don't know how to put your emotions into words. Maybe you're the opposite of the naturally shy type and tend to speak up for yourself whenever you feel like it. However, you do so in a way that aggravates or offends everyone around you. If someone says something you don't like, you blow up and get emotional. As a result, you fail to speak your mind effectively and all the other person hears is a tirade of emotion that doesn't make any sense. This may hinder you from resolving conflicts calmly and effectively. You may think that shouting others down or interrupting them is a sign of your superiority, but the truth is that you are simply destroying whatever social capital you may have in the long run.

This is where the *Assertive Wizard* comes in. This book is a straightforward guide that shows you how to behave, speak, and act when communicating with others or expressing your thoughts and emotions. We often assume that our social skills are good enough to get us ahead in life, but the truth is that there is always room for improvement. This book will show you how to leverage the right communication skills to advance yourself in the workspace. You will also discover how to communicate with friends and family in a way that is wholesome and socially uplifting for everyone concerned.

You will learn the importance of assertiveness and why being self-confident matters. I will share with you some practical ways of boosting your confidence and assertiveness. You will also learn about emotional intelligence and the role it plays in your communication skills. Though more emphasis is usually placed on intellect, this book will help you understand why your emotional competence also matters. I will share tools and tips that can help you become a more impactful communicator in any setting so that you are prepared to speak effectively to any kind of audience.

You will also discover how to adopt the right attitude — of passion and enthusiasm — when communicating your message. You will learn how to tap into your inner motivation so that you can deeply connect with others and ultimately inspire them to do the same. I will teach you the art of negotiation and how to subtly influence others through words as well as body language. This is going to make a huge difference in your influence at the workplace. Finally, I'm going to demonstrate how you can speak with greater impact so that your message always resonates with your audience.

By the time you finish reading this book, you'll know how to be more assertive and develop the kind of confident communication skills that build your social net worth and network.

But who am I, and why should you take seriously the ideas that I share with you in this book?

I am Marlene Gonzalez, the founder and president of LCG Group LLC. I am involved in leadership development and executive coaching. I'm also a certified executive coach and licensed practitioner for Insights Discovery North America. In my line of work, I partner with organizations to inspire and transform their employees so that they can overcome professional challenges and succeed.

I have held several executive positions in corporations all across the United States, Europe, and Latin America. I also served as Senior Director of Global Training, Learning, and Development for McDonald's Corporation. Throughout my career, I have discovered that confident and assertive communication skills are necessary for transformational leadership. I understand the importance of assertiveness and confidence when communicating. This book is one way for me to share what I've learned coaching countless leaders so that you too can be successful and reach your personal and professional goals.

You have a lot to gain by being more assertive and self-confident. There's no need to be afraid of speaking in public or even fearing confrontation. Just like the lion in *The Wizard of Oz*, you already have the courage within you. All you need now are some practical tools and inspiration to set you on your path. You don't have to lose emotional control every time you express yourself. You can learn to be assertive without being aggressive.

Let's face it. At some point, you will find yourself in a situation where you need to communicate assertively and confidently to get what you want in life. Let me show you how you can prepare to handle such opportunities so that you can boldly grab them with both hands.

If you've ever wanted to boost your confidence, be more assertive and improve your communication skills, then this is the book for you. With its help, you can do it!

1

TAKE A STAND FOR YOURSELF

We live in a world where it is deemed okay to be outwardly aggressive toward others, especially when it comes to chasing our notions of success. On the other hand, despite the drawbacks of needless aggression, you also have to admit that being passive easily leads to disappointment and frustration. In such a society, you need to learn how to avoid these extremes, be confident, and stand up for yourself. In this chapter, you will discover what it means to be assertive and why it is so important to develop a healthy level of self-confidence. These two concepts are intricately intertwined, and you will discover how to leverage their power to become a better communicator.

But before we go any further, you first need to understand what being assertive means and why you should cultivate assertiveness in your life.

WHAT IS ASSERTIVENESS?

Assertiveness can be defined as calmly and confidently standing up for your rights without being either aggressive or passive. It means expressing your thoughts and feelings directly and honestly while still respecting the rights of others. When you are assertive, you are not afraid of sharing your opinions, desires, and beliefs as you interact with others. Whether it's in the workplace or at home, you stand up for your own best interests without feeling anxious, upsetting others, or even getting upset yourself. You encourage others to share their views openly and honestly so that your interactions are wholesome and appropriate for everyone involved.

But as mentioned earlier, if you are not assertive, you are likely to display either passivity or aggression.

Most of us were raised to be nice and polite. We were taught that it was in our best interests to be caring, put others first, avoid conflict, and try to make others feel good. But in his bestselling book, *Not Nice*, Dr. Aziz Gazipura argues to the contrary. He contends that most people who act nice end up feeling frustrated and anxious because they sacrifice their authentic selves just to please others. They find it difficult to stand up for themselves because they believe that if they do, other people won't like them. In other words, being nice can be a cage that traps you in a life of guilt and fear.

On the opposite end of the spectrum is the aggressive individual. While we all tend to act aggressively once in a while, this is usually an indication that you lack self-confidence and are trying to compensate by imposing your will on others. Aggressive behavior is usually characterized by hostility and force. This kind of attacking behavior is used to cause fear or pain to others so that you can have your way. This should not be entertained during regular social interactions in the workplace or at home. The only time you should seriously consider showing aggressive behavior is when you are being physically threatened and need to ward off the danger.

But what exactly are the characteristics that separate aggression from assertiveness?

AGGRESSION VS. ASSERTIVENESS

There is a world of difference between being assertive and aggressive. Yet, for some reason, an aggressive style of communication is often misconstrued as being assertive. Most people believe that assertiveness means being pushy and getting your way over others. At the same time, it is easy to confuse someone's assertiveness for aggressiveness or arrogance. But assertiveness is not the same thing as aggression, and there are specific traits that define each of these behaviors.

Here are some examples to further describe the differences between the two. As you read, ask yourself which traits you tend to display more often during your social interactions.

1. **Expression** – Assertiveness is a positive expression where you know your value and are not afraid of expressing your opinions. You also honor others and are considerate of their ideas. Aggression is a negative expression that involves disregarding other people's desires and making them feel undervalued.
2. **Responsibility** – An assertive person accepts their responsibilities, can admit to their mistakes, and is quick to apologize. They also don't have a problem delegating and letting

others shine. An aggressive person, however, struggles to take responsibility for their actions. They would rather blame someone else and never apologize for any mistakes. They also have a problem delegating because they want to appear superior all the time.

3. **Respect** – Assertiveness is founded on respecting others as equals. However, an aggressive person does not respect the rights of other people. They communicate in a way that disrespects the thoughts, feelings, and beliefs of others, thus undermining their sense of self-esteem.

4. **Language and Tone** – An assertive person uses descriptive language and a balanced tone of voice when explaining their opinions. This ensures that whatever they are saying is clear and not misconstrued as judgment or condemnation. An aggressive person tends to rely on attacking language because they do not have the right communication skills to get their message across. They raise their voice needlessly to dominate a conversation, thus displaying their lack of emotional control.

5. **Fairness** – Assertiveness leads to a productive or fair outcome. If you are assertive when negotiating a deal, you generally want everyone

involved to win. Aggression, on the other hand, leads to unfairness and causes things to go downhill. If you are aggressive, you put your interests above everyone else's. You have an insatiable need to win, and for you to win, other people have to lose.

6. **Feedback** – An assertive person is always asking for feedback so that they can fine-tune their ideas and achieve a compromise. They are also not afraid of criticism. When conflicts arise, they offer constructive feedback that resolves the situation amicably. An aggressive person rarely asks for feedback and does not like receiving criticism. They have a fragile ego and are afraid of someone poking holes in their ideas. When they do offer feedback, they do so in a way that creates or escalates tension.

7. **Dominance** – Assertive people are confident in themselves and do not feel the need to dominate a relationship. Since they don't feel it is necessary to show their superiority, they generally seek out other assertive people. Aggressive people seek to dominate others and want to feel superior in a relationship. This explains why they usually look for passive individuals to associate with so that they can

have someone to dominate. They use aggressive behavior to instill fear and passivity in others.

After reading through these descriptions, you should be able to know which communication style you normally use. Remember that self-awareness is the first step toward changing a behavior, so make sure that you are honest with yourself. This will help you reap the maximum benefits from this book.

BENEFITS OF BEING ASSERTIVE

There are many benefits to being assertive, both in the workplace and at home. They include:

Enhanced Self-awareness and Confidence

This is probably the biggest benefit of assertiveness. When you act assertively in your life, you gain a greater awareness of who you are and the value that you bring to those around you. If you are a parent, you'll find it easier to discern the innate traits of your child and help them become self-aware as well. At work, your self-confidence will enable you to become more productive and effective.

Better Managerial Aptitude

An assertive manager treats every employee with respect and fairness, and they expect the same from everyone else. As a result, their colleagues trust and open up to them. This creates an atmosphere that fosters growth and transformation for all.

Better Negotiating Skills

When you are assertive, you always try to find a solution that is best for all parties involved. You recognize the value of people and their ideas and finding a win-win solution makes you a great negotiator.

Competent Problem-solving

Apart from feeling confident in your abilities, being assertive creates the need to go the extra mile to find workable solutions whenever a problem arises. You overcome the tendency to hide (passivity) or find someone to blame (aggression).

Stress Management

By being assertive, you develop a high level of self-assurance that prevents you from succumbing to stress and anxiety, especially when things don't go according to plan.

Job Satisfaction

Nobody wants to go to a job where they feel devalued and disrespected every day. Being assertive helps you set the right boundaries and earn the respect of peers and superiors alike. You will then enjoy your time at work.

WHY ASSERTIVENESS MATTERS

Some may argue that being aggressive is the right way for them to communicate and socialize with others. Maybe they've seen positive results from their past aggressive behavior. Others may even contend that passivity (i.e., going along to get along) has its merits. However, there are many reasons why being assertive is the best way to relate and communicate with others.

Assertiveness shows others that you respect yourself. When people see that, they respond by showing you respect. If you're a pushover, nobody takes you seriously. If you're a bulldozer, others will resent you. Being assertive allows you to confidently stand up for your interests while also allowing others the right to argue for their own. Furthermore, when you use an assertive communication style, it becomes easier to deliver your message to people as clearly as possible. There is none of the confusion that characterizes a passive communicator or the stress and fear that is synonymous with an aggressive communicator.

There is one other important point to remember about assertiveness. You should view it as the balance point between passivity and aggression. To be assertive means knowing which situations to accept and which ones to resist so that you avoid being manipulated. This is a skill that you have to learn well.

TIPS FOR PRACTICING ASSERTIVENESS

Being assertive is a social and communication skill that anyone can learn. However, transitioning from passivity or aggression to assertiveness is not easy to do for most people. The truth is that some are not naturally predisposed to being assertive. Others find themselves living or working in an environment where being aggressive is openly encouraged. Regardless of your situation, here are seven steps you can take to help you develop your assertiveness:

1. **Improve Your Understanding of Yourself –** This will help you see your value to the team, organization, and social circle. When you understand yourself, you realize that you deserve dignity and respect just like everyone else. This allows you to set boundaries that suit your needs.
2. **Set Clear Goals and Voice Them to Others –**

One of the challenges that passive people face is that they expect others to recognize their needs and help them achieve those. This approach doesn't work. You need to identify your goals, then tell your colleagues, friends, or family what you need from them to achieve those goals. As you confidently stand up for your goals, make sure that the request you're making doesn't cause the other person to sacrifice their needs. You want them to help you, so find a way to make it a win-win situation.

3. **Don't Apologize for Your Assertiveness –** When you act assertively, some people may become resentful. Do not take it personally or shrink back from the situation. You cannot control how people respond to you. Simply acknowledge their behavior, keep your cool, and always act respectfully.
4. **Speak Your Truth –** There are times when you'll face people who challenge your rights and act negatively toward you. When this happens, don't be afraid to confront them and speak what's on your mind. Yes, it's okay to get angry when dealing with negative people or issues. The important thing is to express your emotions constructively and respectfully rather than bottle them up or lose control.

5. **Practice Saying "No"** – If you have spent most of your life being passive, it can be very difficult to say no to people. But this is something that you must do to develop your assertiveness. Start with small things, for example, when a friend tells you to pick something up for them that forces you to go out of your way to do it. If you can't find a win-win scenario, then just refuse. Being a people-pleaser may seem like the noble thing to do, but it ultimately makes you feel powerless over your own life.

6. **Use Assertive Statements or Words** – One of the most powerful words in existence is "I". When you use statements like "I want …" or "I feel …," you come across as assertive. The other person pays attention to what you're saying and is likely to respect your boundaries. Furthermore, you can also use direct and emphatic verbs when stating your position. For example, say "I will go to …" rather than "I should go to …". Instead of saying "I have to …," say "I choose to …"

7. **Use Body Language** – Non-verbal communication can be just as powerful as words. Body language such as a straight posture, acting confident even when you're not, maintaining eye contact, and a neutral or

positive facial expression are all ways of displaying assertiveness.

These tips won't make you assertive overnight. However, they will help you start the journey toward standing up for yourself. You should practice them continually until you start to see the kind of changes you want in your life.

WHY SELF-CONFIDENCE MATTERS

As you have seen in the previous section, assertiveness is closely connected to self-confidence. If you are confident, you are more likely to act assertively. This happens whether you do it intentionally or not. At the same time, being assertive will boost your confidence, thus creating a positive cycle that works in your favor. However, do not confuse this with a sense of self-importance because that may lead to aggressive behavior.

But why is self-confidence so important?

If you examine the lives of individuals who have poor social or communication skills, you will realize they lack self-confidence. This is because self-confidence plays a major role in your behavior and communication style. When you feel good about yourself and your skills, it becomes easier to socialize with others and work successfully within a team. Self-confidence also allows you to communicate more effectively in a way that is direct and clear. You will say what you mean and mean what you say. This enables people to respect and understand you better.

Now that you understand what it means to be self-confident and why it's important, let's clarify something. Many people tend to confuse self-confidence with self-esteem. These may sound like the same thing, but they are slightly different in terms of conceptualization.

SELF-CONFIDENCE VS. SELF-ESTEEM

Self-esteem is a personal evaluation of your worth or value. It is based on how much you like or appreciate yourself and involves the way you perceive your appearance, behaviors, and emotions. When you have low self-esteem, you tend to be negative and unmotivated. You are also more likely to assume that others don't like you. This can hurt the way you communicate with people around you. You may even be afraid of socializing with others, and this can cause depression or shyness. On the other hand, people with high self-esteem love themselves as they are and expect others to like them as well. By building your self-esteem, you also boost your confidence and ability to communicate effectively.

When we talk about self-confidence, we are referring to the belief you have in yourself and *your skills or abilities*. Unlike self-esteem, this has less to do with your worth and more to do with your performance. While it is true that having high self-esteem can translate into self-confidence, this isn't always the case. The good news is that having high self-esteem and self-confidence increase your chances of enjoying positive relationships.

Since self-confidence is related to performance, there are specific factors that may influence how confident you feel about your abilities. These include:

- **Prior experience and performance** – When you accomplish a task, you are likely to be confident in your ability to succeed in that task again.
- **Experience of others** – If you see someone doing a task successfully, you can know whether you can accomplish the same thing.
- **Social association** – If you see a peer at work performing a task, then you may feel confident in your ability to do the same task. This is

especially true if you share similar traits to the other individual.
- **Social encouragement** – When you receive encouragement from someone you trust, you feel more confident in your abilities.
- **Self-encouragement** – There are times when nobody is there to encourage you. You have to learn to rely on your positive self-talk to boost your confidence.

BENEFITS OF SELF-CONFIDENCE

Self-confidence is a vital element in living a happy and fulfilled life. When you have a good grasp of its benefits, you will be inspired to take the steps necessary to develop greater self-confidence in your life. Here are nine benefits of self-confidence:

Less Fear and Anxiety

Being confident in yourself empowers you to have the courage to try new things. You are no longer a slave to the fear and anxiety that hold back so many people. You'll be more willing to go for that promotion or ask that attractive stranger out on a date. When you are less fearful and anxious, your self-talk also becomes less negative. One of the biggest problems that most people suffer is excessive mulling over the past. You find yourself replaying past mistakes, old broken relationships, failed jobs, etc. This kind of negative thinking induces stress, anxiety, and depression. But when you improve your self-confidence, you can replace the negative mindset with a positive one.

Motivated Life

Success breeds confidence and self-confidence generates motivation and success in life. When you are self-confident, you feel motivated to go out into the world and accomplish great things. These don't have to be big tasks that draw the adulation of others. It can be small accomplishments that push your limits every day, such as achieving a fitness goal, learning a new skill, or even overcoming a personal challenge. Confidence inspires you to get out of your comfort zone and perform tasks that may be scary. However, you do them anyway because your motivation is stronger than your fear.

Fulfilling Relationships

If you lack self-confidence when you approach strangers, you automatically focus more on yourself than on anyone else. Your perception is negative, so you assume that people are also thinking negative things about you. This prevents you from establishing close relationships with others, and the result is that others will not be attracted to you. However, when you are confident in who you are, you walk into that room not worried about what others think. Since you aren't caught up in negativity and wrong assumptions, you are more open to engaging with others. The more you enjoy talking and meeting new people in a relaxed state, the more they will enjoy being around you. Your self-confidence will also help you become a more empathetic individual, thus enabling you to create deeper connections.

Greater Sense of Self

Being confident in yourself means you have come to know, love, and accept yourself as you are. You are no longer wearing a mask, trying to be someone you're not just to fit in with the crowd. This puts you in touch with your *authentic self*, which is the real version of you. Self-confidence enables you to accept your flaws and work on improving them in a non-judgmental way. It also helps you celebrate your strengths and use them to achieve your purpose.

Improved Resilience

Setbacks and challenges are all part of normal life, and everyone experiences failure regardless of confidence level. However, those who have high self-confidence tend to bounce back better from failure than those who have low confidence in themselves. Being confident allows you to judge situations objectively and keep moving forward despite the presence of obstacles. This builds your mental resilience and reduces your fear of making mistakes or taking risks. As a result, you also end up succeeding more often.

Stress Management

Imagine standing in front of a room full of people as you prepare to give a presentation or perform a play. The pressure you're feeling is likely to be overwhelming. At such a moment, you need to be confident if you want to control your stress and anxiety. A high level of self-confidence helps you perform your best under pressure.

Social Influence

It is much easier to influence others around you when you project self-confidence. People naturally gravitate to those who appear self-assured. This can be an effective strategy when attracting a mate, selling a product, or negotiating a raise.

Leadership Potential

Great leaders and executives have a massive presence that they convey due to their high level of self-confidence. Your confidence tells others that you have the potential to lead and solve problems head-on. It's also a well-known fact that confident employees are more likely to be promoted than those who are not.

Sexual Attractiveness

When someone is searching for a mate, they will naturally look for signs of self-confidence. This tells them that you are willing to stand up for yourself – and them. It also says that you are comfortable being yourself.

EXERCISES FOR BUILDING SELF-CONFIDENCE

It should be clear by now that self-confidence allows you to achieve your personal and professional goals much more effectively. You may not have much self-confidence right now, but you can change that by utilizing particular techniques. You've probably heard of tips such as looking into the mirror and telling yourself "I am confident" repeatedly until you feel confident. This strategy may work for some people, but I believe that there are more effective suggestions that you can use. Here are eight practical ways of boosting your self-confidence:

1. **Positive Self-talk** – There is always an inner voice in your mind speaking to you. The sad

truth is that we often allow this voice to say negative things about ourselves. Since your mind doesn't differentiate self-talk from reality, you can easily chip away at your self-confidence using negative words. However, you can consciously reverse this and create a positive internal dialogue. In your quiet moments, use some positive self-talk to encourage yourself. Your subconscious will listen to the positive message and trigger a boost in self-confidence.

2. **Visualization** – Your imagination is a powerful tool in your arsenal when it comes to creating your reality. By visualizing a positive outcome, your subconscious believes it is real, making it more likely to occur. Let's say that you are fearful about having a conversation with a family member about the way they've been disrespecting you. Sit down and imagine everything you would say, then visualize them responding positively to you. Imagine the conversation ending with a positive outcome that suits you. This will give you the confidence to approach the other person.

3. **Take More Risks** – When you make a plan to perform a task, there is a chance that you may fail at whatever you intend to accomplish.

However, taking risks is how you learn and gain confidence in your abilities. By consistently stepping out of your comfort zone, you gradually expand your risk tolerance. The new changes and challenges help to develop your confidence because you're focusing on the process more than the outcome. Think about talking to a stranger, trying a new restaurant, or confronting somebody you normally avoid. Even small successes can build up your confidence over time.

4. **Know Thyself** – Self-awareness is a core part of your self-confidence. You should understand what your strengths and weaknesses are so that you know what to focus on. By paying attention to your strengths, you improve your self-confidence. At the same time, being aware of your weaknesses allows you to work on them. Developing these weak areas also improves your confidence.

5. **Positive Social Circle** – The people you spend time with can either elevate your self-confidence and esteem or bring you down with negativity. There are too many negative people intent on demoralizing and devaluing others. If you have such people in your social circle, it's time to find new friends. You should associate

more with people who build your self-confidence. If you have family members who are persistently destroying your self-esteem, simply limit the time you spend with them.

6. **Increase Your Skill Level** – When you develop and master a certain skill, you become extremely self-confident in that field. Spend more time studying and practicing a skill so that you become more competent than the majority of people. If it's playing an instrument, spend an extra hour practicing. If you want to improve your public speaking skills, then consider taking a class. Confidence comes from competence.

7. **Change Your Body Image** – This may be as simple as changing your grooming habits, buying a new set of clothes, or starting an exercise routine. You may be surprised how confident you feel after a shower, shave, and putting on some nice clothes. The clothes don't have to be expensive. The important thing is that they make you feel good about yourself. Studies show that wearing different clothes from what you're used to can make you act or think differently. Finally, you can start working out to develop the kind of physique you desire. Exercise can help you lose weight, build muscle,

and improve your mood. Every workout session you complete is another accomplishment to be proud of, and this boosts your self-confidence.

8. **Walk and Sit Straight** – There is no point in dressing well and working out only to walk around with your head down and back bent. Learn to walk and sit with a straight posture, and this will make you feel more confident.

Working on your self-confidence is a lifelong journey. The information you have discovered in this chapter should be enough to get you started. If you follow the steps outlined here, you will experience positive changes to your communication style and behavior. As your assertiveness and self-confidence grow, you will become a more emotionally intelligent individual.

2

EMOTIONAL INTELLIGENCE 101

There is no denying the importance of emotions when it comes to your ability to effectively communicate with other people. As you've already discovered, assertiveness means controlling your emotions so that you express yourself clearly and fearlessly. In this chapter, you will discover what emotional intelligence is and how it influences your communication skills. You will also gain insight into the different aspects of emotional intelligence and how you can test and improve your emotional quotient.

For a long time, we have been told that what the world needs is highly intellectual people. Yet, with all the focus on intellect and the advancements humanity has made thus far, we are still struggling to get along with one another. While it's true that being smart gives you a good chance of attaining success, it is not enough for achieving a fulfilled life. As you are about to learn, emotional intelligence plays a huge part in unlocking your personal and professional potential.

WHAT IS EMOTIONAL INTELLIGENCE?

In simple terms, emotional intelligence refers to your ability to identify your feelings and those of others and then using that information to guide your thoughts and actions. More holistically, we define it as your ability to recognize, utilize, and manage your emotions in a way that allows you to empathize with others, communicate effectively, overcome challenges, relieve stress, and resolve conflict. A high level of emotional intelligence heightens your awareness of what you're saying, how you're saying it, and how the other person is interpreting the message.

Going by these definitions, it should be clear that not everyone has the same level of emotional intelligence. You have probably met people who are very tuned into their feelings and can cope better with the different challenges that life throws at them. On the other hand, you must have also come across people who are so unaware of their own emotions that they are unable to communicate well or form good relationships.

Emotional intelligence is determined by measuring your emotional quotient (EQ). This is a measure of how emotionally intelligent you are depending on your score on a standardized test. The higher your score, the higher your EQ. While some think that your EQ is inborn, others argue that there are things you can do to learn and strengthen your emotional intelligence. Your level of emotional intelligence can generally be defined by four attributes:

Self-management

This means you can control your impulsive emotions and actions and have healthy outlets for regulating your feelings. When you take on a task, you stay committed to it, yet quickly adapt to unforeseen changes.

Self-awareness

This means you understand your emotions and how they influence your thoughts and actions. You recognize your strengths and weaknesses and are confident in your abilities.

Social Awareness

This means that you are empathetic and understand the needs and emotions of those around you. You easily identify their emotional cues and feel comfortable socializing within a group.

Relationship Management

This means you can develop and maintain strong relationships where you communicate effectively, influence others, and defuse conflict.

IMPORTANCE OF EMOTIONAL INTELLIGENCE

As mentioned before, having a high IQ does not guarantee fulfillment in life. You also need a high EQ to better cope with the ups and downs of life as well as build the right kind of relationships. Emotional intelligence has so much practical utility that it affects every area of your personal and professional life.

Your emotional intelligence can affect how well you perform at school or in the workplace. These are two places where you need high emotional intelligence to navigate a complex social construct. Individuals with a high EQ make better leaders and can inspire others to succeed. It is a well-known fact now that most hiring managers gauge potential recruits based on their emotional intelligence because it affects the candidate's ability to fit into the organization's culture.

Another area affected by emotional intelligence is your health. The inability to properly manage your emotions can lead to all kinds of stress and anxiety problems. These can trigger ailments such as high blood pressure, strokes, heart attacks, infertility, immunosuppression, and even accelerated aging. Apart from the physical aspect, poor emotional control can also cause mental health issues. Stress and anxiety can lead to loneliness, social isolation, and depression.

Finally, emotional intelligence influences the quality of your social interactions. When you understand how to control your emotions, it becomes easier to channel and positively express them. You can think before reacting even when faced with a highly charged emotional situation. If an agitated family member confronts you, you can calm tensions by taking some time to think before responding. The same also applies when you're angry at someone you feel has wronged you. Emotional intelligence makes it easier to communicate and empathize with others. You put yourself in their shoes and try to see things from their perspective. This leads to deeper bonds and ensures that you feel a sense of love and community within your social group.

DO I HAVE HIGH EMOTIONAL INTELLIGENCE?

What does emotional intelligence look like in an everyday setting? Some simple signs reflect a person with a high emotional quotient. Use the signs below to gauge your emotional intelligence:

You pause and reflect on your feelings.

Stopping to think before you say or do something isn't as easy as you may believe. Someone may make a comment that riles you or you may be offered what appears to be a great opportunity. However, the smart thing to do in both situations is to take a moment to reflect on the choice you're about to make. This can help you avoid making a bad decision due to a temporary emotion.

You contemplate feelings.

An emotionally intelligent person tends to have a high sense of self and social awareness. They reflect on their emotional strengths and weaknesses and explore how their mood affects their decisions. They also contemplate the emotions of others and ponder about what's going on in their minds.

You try to manage your thoughts.

At any given moment, you are experiencing some kind of emotion. These emotions then trigger specific thoughts which lead you to behave a certain way. Therefore, to control your actions you must start by controlling your emotions. This is not an easy thing to do. The only solution is to control your thoughts so that regardless of your feelings, you always stay in control of your responses. This prevents you from being enslaved by your emotions.

You don't take criticism personally.

Criticism and negative feedback can be tough to accept. Being emotionally intelligent allows you to reframe the negative words and use them to your advantage. Instead of getting emotional, use the criticism to learn about the person giving the negative feedback. Ask yourself why they are criticizing you. It may be that they are genuine and have a desire to correct you. If so, use their feedback to become a better person. If they are being vindictive, maybe it's a sign that you shouldn't associate closely with them or take them too seriously.

You are true to yourself.

Assertiveness is a major sign of an individual with a high EQ. When you say something, you mean it. You always stick to your principles and are authentic with those who share your values. Though some people may not appreciate your authenticity, you always stay true to who you are.

You praise and give others constructive feedback.

We all desire to be appreciated for who we are and what we do. By focusing on the positive aspects of others, you build trust and inspire them to be better.

Your appreciation of others is specific rather than vague, which shows that you're not merely pandering to their emotions. Even when you do criticize, you do so in a constructive way. This allows the recipient to perceive the feedback positively.

You let go of the past.

An emotionally intelligent person doesn't hold onto resentment because it prevents healing from taking place. Refusing to forgive and forget keeps you in emotional bondage, thus preventing your progress in life.

You protect yourself from emotional manipulation.

There are people out there who are eager to manipulate the emotions of others for selfish gain. By continually improving your emotional intelligence, you can avoid falling for such traps.

You are comfortable apologizing.

We all make mistakes that affect others from time to time. Unfortunately, most people have a problem with saying they are sorry. Refusing to apologize is a sign that you're putting your ego above your relationships with others. Even if you're not wrong, apologizing lets others know that you value the relationship. By displaying such humility, you attract others to you and build quality relationships.

You show empathy.

Emotional intelligence is connected to your ability to see the world through the eyes of others. You can connect to the thoughts and emotions of others without judging them. Though you may have a difference of opinion, you can still understand people and build a deeper bond with them.

MEASURING EMOTIONAL INTELLIGENCE

There are several methods used to test a person's EQ. Unlike a standard intelligence quotient (IQ) test with right and wrong answers, EQ tests give you options. The test provides several potentially correct responses, and you are graded based on how you justify your answer. There are two categories of tests that are used to measure emotional intelligence:

- Performance Tests
- Self-reporting Tests

Performance Tests

These are also known as ability tests and are administered like IQ tests. You are required to respond to a particular situation, then your abilities are assessed by a third party. For example, you may be asked to look at images of different people and identify the emotion shown on their faces. Your performance is determined by how other respondents have performed in the same test. Two specific measurements are used under this type of test: MSCEIT and ESCI.

MSCEIT (Mayer-Salovey-Caruso Emotional Intelligence Test) is commonly used in coaching and academic research to measure a person's unique emotional knowledge and awareness. Though it is extremely rigorous and objective, it is also very time-consuming. The MSCEIT test focuses on four key areas:

- *Emotional Perception* – This is your ability to perceive your emotional state as well as non-verbal cues from others, such as body language and facial expressions.
- *Emotional Reasoning* – Once you perceive an emotion, you must have the ability to use it to trigger some cognitive activity. You need to prioritize your thoughts and actions based on the emotion perceived, especially if you are dealing with a problem.
- *Emotional Understanding* – The test measures your ability to interpret the probable cause of a particular emotion and its underlying meaning.

For example, when your partner speaks to you harshly, you may rush to assume that they are displeased with something you've done. However, they may have had a tough day at work with their overbearing boss and they are just angry at their work performance.
- *Emotional Management* – At this stage, the test measures how well you manage your emotions.

As you can see, the four areas are arranged according to complexity. The first two are the most basic stages while the latter ones are at a higher level of emotional intelligence.

ESCI (Emotional and Social Competency Inventory) is an older test than the MSCEIT. It involves both a self-assessment questionnaire and assessments from people who know you well. These can be friends, family members, work colleagues, classmates, supervisors, etc. The goal is to get a 360-degree perspective by taking into account others' perception of your emotional intelligence and comparing it with your own. For example, you may see yourself as a very sociable person. But after the opinions of others are accounted for, you may be surprised to realize that you are deficient in empathy and emotional control. This is a good test for determining which individuals can best serve as team leaders and managers. Some of the areas that the ESCI test focuses on include self-control, self-awareness, adaptability, empathy, organizational awareness, conflict management, influence, and teamwork.

Self-reporting Tests

This is the easiest test to administer and score so it is more commonly used. You are expected to respond to questions or statements based on specific topics, for example, self-perception and social interactions. One of the tools used under the self-reporting test is the Emotional Quotient Inventory (EQ-i). This is the oldest EQ tool ever published and adopted globally. This test compares your results to other respondents within your geographical location and culture. This makes sure that the results are valid and reliable.

The EQ-i focuses on five different categories of your social and emotional intelligence:

1. **Intra-personal** – How well do you understand and manage yourself? This is based on your self-regard, assertiveness, independence, and self-actualization.
2. **Inter-personal** – How well do you socialize with other people? This is based on your ability to sustain close relationships, cooperate with, and contribute to others.

3. **Adaptability** – This is based on your realism, problem-solving skills, and flexibility.
4. **Stress Management** – Do you stay calm under difficult situations and resist the urge to react prematurely? This is based on your ability to tolerate stress and control your impulses.
5. **General Mood** – This is based on your ability to be optimistic and happy. You are tested on whether you can stay positive under adverse conditions. You are also tested on your enthusiasm and ability to enjoy life.

There's one important aspect of the EQ-i test that you should note. Of the five categories tested, only one has the power to influence all the others. This is your *general mood*. If you are the kind of person who knows how to stay optimistic and happy regardless of your external conditions, you'll find it much easier to master the other four areas. You will be able to improve all your relationships, become more adaptable, and manage your stress.

EMOTIONAL INTELLIGENCE AND EMOTIONAL COMPETENCE

These two concepts are intricately linked both theoretically and practically. However, they are not identical.

Earlier in the chapter, we defined emotional intelligence as the ability to identify your emotions and those of others as a basis for guiding your thoughts and actions. Emotional competence, however, is the ability to recognize and express your emotions freely when interacting with other people. Whereas emotional intelligence is the interplay between your emotions and intelligence, emotional competence is a skill that you use during social interactions (Seal & Andrews-Brown, 2010). Based on the name, emotional intelligence is linked to your cognitive ability while emotional competence is linked to your performance.

Think of emotional intelligence as a vast array of cognitive abilities with emotional competence simply being one aspect or expression. Whereas emotional intelligence focuses on your ability to manage your emotions, emotional competence focuses on how to appropriately express those emotions.

But these two concepts do share some factors. The most important one is self-awareness. For example, as a child grows, so does their cognitive ability and self-awareness. The child naturally gains a greater level of emotional intelligence which is also inspired by their cultural socialization. As their emotional intelligence increases, they gain a greater capacity to identify and manage their emotions. However, they still have a long way to go before they can develop emotional competence.

Think of a naturally talented singer. They may have the potential to be a superstar someday, but will they become successful if they don't practice? No! They must learn and develop their talent to use it effectively. They have to put in the work the same way a child has to go through a diverse range of social experiences to develop their emotional competence.

Studies show that there are health problems related to a lack of emotional competence. When you bottle your emotions instead of expressing them, you may end up suffering from mental as well as physical ailments such as fatigue, rapid weight gain or loss, and hypertension. Your relationships may also deteriorate due to emotional incompetence.

According to research, this can be viewed from a cultural perspective as well. In eastern societies like Japan, there is an emphasis on collectivism, which means you're naturally encouraged to express your emotions. Children in such countries are raised to be emotionally competent. However, going by their high suicide rates, it would be more prudent to train Japanese children in emotional intelligence so that they can better manage their emotions. In western societies where individualism is emphasized, people have learned how to manage their emotions. Since they already have emotional intelligence, American children would benefit more from developing their emotional competence. This would allow them to freely express these emotions in a healthy way (Hayashi, Karasawa, and Tobin (2009)).

HOW TO COMMUNICATE YOUR EMOTIONS EFFECTIVELY

What do you do when you realize that your emotional competence is holding you back from achieving the results you desire? I have provided three practical steps on how to communicate your emotions more effectively below:

Step One: Identify Your Emotions

The first step in communicating your emotions is to identify them. You need to open up and be honest with yourself about whatever feelings you may be experiencing. Only after you have done this can you talk about those feelings with another person. This is more challenging than it sounds because we have very effective defense mechanisms that hide our emotions from our conscious minds.

How many times have you said to yourself that you're just having a bad day but never did any further soul-searching to find out why? This is one of the many ways you block yourself from identifying your underlying emotions. So what should you do to discover your feelings? Here are some ideas:

Take Your Emotional Temperature

Get a notebook and ask yourself the following questions:

- What feelings am I experiencing right now?
- Which one do I feel the most?
- When did this feeling arise?

Include as much detail as possible as you write down the answers to these questions. Don't be afraid to ask yourself even deeper questions, and as you do, try to rate the level of pleasantness or unpleasantness of the emotion. You should also rate your energy level in terms of whether you feel excited, relaxed, lethargic, or nervous. You may be surprised at just how much information comes through during this process.

Identify Your Stressors

In your notebook, write down all the stressors that you think could be triggering the emotion. Think about any events that may have occurred. For example, you could be sad due to a loss or the memory of a past loss. If you're a student, you may feel anxious because you're contemplating your future career choices. Examine your home and professional life to discern any patterns that may be affecting your relationships or work. Try to avoid the tendency to judge or chastise yourself for feeling the way you do.

Talk About Your Emotions

The worst thing you can do is to try to stifle your emotions. This is something we often do out of fear. By talking about your feelings, you diminish them and their impact on your life. If you are angry, confront that emotion to reduce its intensity. It only gets worse if you ignore it.

Step Two: Interpret and Perceive

Your ability to correctly interpret and perceive the emotions of others is one of the factors that affect your behavior in relationships. More often than not, the way you perceive and interpret an event is very different from the event itself. While you may assume that you're responding to what a person said, you instead are responding to your interpretation of their words. This happens so fast that you rarely know that it's happening. Therefore, when your emotional response does not match the event, you have to explore the situation further to gain a clearer perspective. Some of the misleading interpretations you should watch out for include:

- *Dichotomous Thinking* – You perceive events to be either of two extremes with no gray areas whatsoever. For example, a dinner date was either delightful or catastrophic.
- *Excessive Personalization* – You interpret someone's mood as your fault. For example, your husband is in a foul mood, and you quickly assume you are the cause.
- *Over-generalization* – You take one negative outcome and expand its impact beyond its scope. For example, your boss asks you to rewrite a report, and you conclude that you're a terrible employee.
- *Filtering* – You focus solely on the negative remarks and forget all the previous positive ones. For example, your teacher criticizes your essay, and you forget all the other positive things she said about your writing in the past.
- *Emotional Reasoning* – You interpret your feelings as evidence of truth. For example, you get dumped and now you're telling yourself that you don't deserve to be in a happy relationship.

Step Three: Express Yourself

The way you express your emotions is a product of your culture and family values. We have all been taught to either hide our feelings or engage in confrontational behavior. However, it is still possible to follow your cultural values and also express yourself in a way that is sensitive to your own needs. You don't always have to express your emotions in a way that exacerbates the situation.

One healthy way to express your emotions is through creative expression. Find some form of creativity and use it to express whatever emotions you feel. You can use writing, drawing, pottery, etc. Research shows that art therapy helps deal with trauma and enhances your mood (Malchiodi, 2012). You can also practice mindfulness and gratitude meditations as part of your daily morning routine.

Another effective way to express your emotions, especially when angry, is to change your words and tone. When someone does or says something that angers you, pause for a minute to reflect on the feeling. Then find a word that reflects your feelings but isn't defensive. Say something like "I feel sad about…" and then explain to them why you feel that way. Be specific about how you feel and the role the other person is playing in triggering that feeling.

You may be thinking that it's only socially awkward geeks or nerds that need to improve their emotional intelligence. However, everyone needs to recognize their deficiencies and work to raise their EQ. You may have the ability to manage your emotions, and yet be terrible at empathizing and reading people's emotional cues. Maybe you're good at socializing but have poor emotional control. You could have a high level of self-awareness but don't know how to maintain long-term relationships or resolve conflict. No matter where you are on the EQ spectrum, you always have room for growth and improvement.

It should be clear by now that although everyone has the potential to be emotionally intelligent, you must develop the ability to use it during your social interactions. Therefore, if you can properly manage your emotions, you can also develop emotional competence through self-discipline. The initial step is to develop emotional intelligence as a foundation and then start building up your emotional competencies. Your emotional intelligence and competence will affect your ability to get your message across when communicating with others.

3

GETTING THE MESSAGE ACROSS

From the moment you were born, you began communicating with the world around you. It may have been in simple cries and grunts, but all you knew was that you were sending a message to those around you. Fast forward to the world you live in now and there's no doubt that communication is the glue that holds all relationships together. Whether it's in the workplace or the home, people have to talk and engage with one another to build rapport and share information. Your ability to communicate effectively determines your success, and this has a huge impact on the trajectory of your career and personal relationships.

In this chapter, you will discover the importance of good communication skills and how to communicate with clarity and impact. You will also discover how to read an audience as well as the techniques you should use when speaking to groups of people.

WHAT IS COMMUNICATION?

In simple terms, communication can be defined as sending and receiving information to achieve understanding. This is usually achieved in multiple ways, but the most common is through the use of words. However, there are other symbols of communication such as body movements, voice tones, and facial expressions. To develop your assertiveness, you must understand the diverse ways people communicate and how to decode their intention. This can be a little confusing especially when it comes to non-verbal communication.

People often use non-verbal communication without knowing it. For example, the way you walk says a lot about you and your mood. You are also communicating a message to people by the clothes you choose to wear. Even nodding your head, though done unconsciously, sends a specific message to people. Therefore, it is important to understand the subtle nuances of communication if you want to create the right kind of impact.

IMPORTANCE OF EFFECTIVE COMMUNICATION SKILLS

With the rise in social media networks, more people are now engaging with one another on a global scale. People who would never have had the chance to communicate with each other can now talk and share information instantly. However, though we can all communicate on some level, not everyone can do so effectively. Let's explore some of the reasons why you need to develop effective communication skills.

The first reason is that communication is related to every process of your life. Everywhere you go and with every social interaction you make, you are communicating a message. It doesn't matter whether you're doing so intentionally or not. Your body language is a powerful form of communication, and even your perceived silence tells people something about you. If this is true, you are better off developing effective communication skills, so you'll have a better chance of sending messages that help rather than hurt you.

Secondly, effective communication brings people closer and enables relationships to be established based on shared principles and values. When you are clear about what you stand for, you can gather a team around you that shares your mindset and vision. You can create an efficient team of colleagues at work or it can even be a group of strangers at a social event.

Communication also shows others that you are knowledgeable and sincere. People can listen to you and decide whether you know what you are talking about. Your ability to communicate well also proves to your audience that you believe in what you are saying. Your sincerity may convince them to put their faith in you.

Finally, having good communication skills enhances your self-confidence. Look at some famous effective communicators and notice just how confident they are. When you learn how to properly get your message across to an audience, you gain even more confidence in yourself. Talking to people and seeing them nod or smile back at you shows that your message is resonating with them. This builds your self-confidence.

The role that communication plays in our daily lives cannot be taken for granted. The world wouldn't be the same without our ability to communicate with each other effectively. Therefore, this is a vital skill that you need to learn well if you want to have a bigger impact in life.

BENEFITS OF EFFECTIVE COMMUNICATION

From a personal and professional standpoint, there are several ways that you benefit from being an effective communicator.

1. It offers people a better insight into who you are and the message you're communicating. It also helps you know how to decode subtle messages from the non-verbal communication of others. This allows you to understand people better.
2. It boosts your chances of getting hired on your terms. When you walk into a job interview, you are expected to present yourself as someone capable of doing the job. However, don't forget that you're also expected to negotiate terms that suit your interests. Though you may get the job, you stand little chance of being hired on *your* terms if you don't articulate your expectations clearly.
3. It helps increase the size of your network. People are naturally drawn to good communicators, so being an effective one enables you to socialize with more people. This also exposes you to more career opportunities.
4. It helps you develop your leadership skills. The

better you become at communicating effectively, the more easily you're able to get your message across. This makes it progressively easier to relate to people and build consensus within a group. This boosts your social position among friends, family, and coworkers.

5. It enables you to maintain good relationships with others even during a tense conversation. When people argue, they stop listening or reading the other person's non-verbal cues. But an effective communicator always focuses on the messages being sent and received. This allows you to avoid ruining your relationships because of petty arguments.
6. It helps you eliminate the waste of time and energy that often characterize poor communication skills. When you cannot communicate effectively, you end up engaging in confusing and anxious conversations. Your non-verbal cues can also send the wrong message to others. This can lead to misunderstandings and guilt.
7. It's the best way to learn. There's no denying that back-and-forth communication is an effective learning tool. People talk to each other so that they can learn from one another.

Nobody espouses this concept better than children. The moment they learn to speak, they ask questions, a lot of questions, because they want to learn. This is why it's recommended for parents to spend time talking to their young children. Communication aids in growth and development.

BARRIERS TO EFFECTIVE COMMUNICATION

To practice effective communication, you must overcome some of the barriers that prevent you from doing so. These include:

Stress

When you feel stressed, you're likely to send out information that is confusing and conflicting. That is why it's difficult to understand someone when they are in a state of panic or intense anxiety. Also, you are likely to misread signals from other people because you're filtering information through your emotional response. To avoid such scenarios, use de-stressing techniques such as deep breathing to calm yourself before engaging in a conversation.

Lack of Focus

Most people still believe that multitasking is a good way to get things done. However, your failure to focus on one thing at a time means you're more likely to ignore or miss an important detail. This is especially significant when you are communicating with another person. If you're scrolling through your computer as you speak to someone or waiting to jump into the conversation with a response, you're going to miss a lot of subtle cues. Effective communication involves paying attention to body language and avoiding distractions.

Body Language

If you're speaking to someone but your body language is conveying something different, the other person is likely to get confused. They may think that you're not being fully sincere with them. You should keep your body language consistent with whatever information you're sharing. There is also the problem of negative body language. When someone is telling you something you don't like, it's easy to find yourself crossing your arms or avoiding eye contact. These cues are a subtle way of telling the person that you don't want to hear what they are saying. Unfortunately, this kind of behavior can trigger the other person to become defensive. Even if you are not particularly enjoying a conversation, avoid using negative body language during verbal interactions.

GUIDELINES FOR EFFECTIVE COMMUNICATION

Though it's simple to define, communication is a complex concept that embodies more than just the exchange of information. You may have succeeded in informing your spouse or co-worker about something you need them to do. But what about the underlying aspects of your message, such as your tone of voice, hand gestures, emotion, or intention? Were you paying attention to these things? How about the mood of the person you were communicating with? To become a better communicator, you should understand all aspects of communication. Here are some general guidelines on the things you need to pay attention to:

Develop Your Listening Skills

There's a difference between listening and hearing. Hearing is a passive approach while listening is more active. Go to a random café and watch how people sitting around a table are conversing. You'll notice that almost everyone has their phone in hand scrolling through messages, yet somehow, they are speaking to one another. They may hear what's being said, but do you think anyone is really listening?

Active listening means paying attention to what's being said and making eye contact with the other person. You have to listen to the subtle tone changes in their voice to understand their emotions. Being a good listener also means asking for clarification if you don't understand something.

Active listening is a powerful communication skill because it creates a deeper connection and shows that you care about what someone is saying. By listening, you can help someone feel understood and even calm them down if they are agitated. To become an active listener, concentrate on the speaker, avoid interrupting them, and show them that you're interested in the conversation. You can express your interest by nodding occasionally or smiling at them.

Understand Non-verbal Cues

Non-verbal cues are an important source of information about a person. By understanding how to read and convey non-verbal signals, you can express yourself better, build stronger bonds, and deal with challenging situations wherever you go. When it comes to reading non-verbal cues, you should consider the differences between individuals, for example, age, culture, gender, religion, and even emotional state. You should also read an individual's non-verbal signals as a whole rather than as single gestures. For example, someone crossing their arms one time doesn't mean they are rebuffing you. Consider all their non-verbal signals as a collective.

When it comes to conveying non-verbal signals, make sure that your body language matches your words. You should also change your non-verbal communication depending on the situation. You shouldn't use the same tone of voice with a child as you would with an adult. If you have to mislead people with your body language, do so in a positive way. For example, if you're nervous on a date, walk into the room smiling with good posture and eye contact.

Manage Stress

Stress is one of those emotional states that can cause you to say something you don't mean. By finding ways to relieve stress and stay calm, you not only avoid making regrettable choices but also help the other person remain calm during a tense interaction. Managing your stress under pressure helps you keep a clear mind so you can communicate effectively. For example, a clear mind is useful when interviewing for a job, presenting a project, or visiting your fiancé's family for the first time.

To communicate effectively in such situations, take time to collect your thoughts before responding. You can use tactics such as asking for a statement to be clarified so you have time to calm yourself. Jumping from one point to another during a conversation may sound as if you're rambling. Make one point, elaborate on it, and then gauge the listener's response before moving on to the next one. When you're done saying something, stop talking. Trying to fill the silence by non-stop talking may expose your nervousness. Another way of relieving stress is to find humor in the situation, especially when the conversation starts to get too serious.

Be Assertive

Assertiveness helps to keep communication clear and also builds your self-esteem. Being assertive when communicating means valuing your opinions as much as you do anyone else's. If you have any negative feedback, try to express it positively and respectfully. It is also important to refuse any request that will allow others to take advantage of you.

There are two forms of assertiveness you can use when communicating. The first is *empathetic assertion*. This is where you recognize the other person's feelings before you state your own needs. Let's say your spouse has been spending too much time at work, including weekends. An empathetic way to show assertiveness would be to say, "I understand you're juggling a lot of projects at work, but I want you to spend more time with your family as well." The second type is *escalating assertion*, where you become increasingly firm with someone if your initial attempts at having your needs met have failed. For example, if a contractor is continually violating a contract, you can threaten to pursue legal action.

Ask Questions

Communication is more enriching if it allows you to know the other person better, and the best way to do so is by asking questions. However, most people are guarded when it comes to revealing their innermost thoughts and feelings. This means you have to find a way to get a person to open up without feeling pressured. The best way to do this is by asking open-ended questions. Instead of asking, "Are you okay?", you can say, "How are you feeling today?" This type of question goes beyond the usual "yes" or "no" and allows someone to share more about themselves if they want to. Asking open-ended questions during conversations breeds more openness and honesty, which then breeds trust. If they don't share much information immediately, be patient, and respect their boundaries.

SPECIFIC GUIDELINES FOR BUSINESS COMMUNICATION

Effective communication is extremely important in every stage of business, whether it's engaging with employees, using new technology, or achieving business goals. Good leaders understand that effective communication leads to effective business results. Though you may already be a great communicator, you can always improve your communication skills. Here are some ideas on how to use communication to achieve your business goals:

1. **Eliminate Assumptions** – Relying on unspoken rules based on assumptions can lead to misunderstandings and financial losses. Just because something happened a certain way in the past doesn't mean it will always be that way. It's best for all parties to communicate their needs and expectations openly every time.
2. **Avoid Visual Aids** – Most business meetings rely on visual aids like PowerPoint presentations. However, it's been shown that visual aids hamper effective communication. Good alternatives include compelling storytelling and non-verbal cues.
3. **Schedule a Good Place and Time to Talk** –

Establish scheduled meetings on a weekly or monthly basis to share relevant information. The location should be quiet with no distractions and the necessary privacy.
4. **Listen Before Talking** – If there's a problem, describe it and how it's affecting your business. Then ask for a solution and wait for a response. Don't begin the conversation by imposing your preferred solution. You should also avoid interrupting the other person while they are talking.
5. **Develop Trust, Integrity, and Credibility** – If an issue comes up, approach others early on and be open about it. You should also show them that you're approachable and truthful.
6. **Acknowledge Positive Behaviors** – If someone takes the time to listen to what you have to say, recognize, and reinforce that behavior by thanking them for their time. This maintains open communication channels.
7. **Be Brief** – In business, time is critical, so be prepared to get someone's attention within the first 15 seconds of a conversation. This will convince them that they need to hear more of what you have to say.
8. **Practice Patience** – You may have some differences with your boss or colleague about

how to get something done. It is okay if you don't always have your way. Business communication should be about strengthening relationships for everyone's benefit and not about winning.

9. **Check for Understanding** – When sharing ideas at a meeting, it's recommended that you over-communicate your message. Most speakers overestimate how much the listeners understand their message. If you're receiving information from someone, ensure that the message has been understood by asking questions and listening keenly.
10. **Understand Your Audience** – If you're leading a team, make sure that you understand your team members well. The more you know about them, the easier it becomes to talk to and spur them to action.

SPECIFIC GUIDELINES FOR COMMUNICATION IN RELATIONSHIPS

Most people believe that talking to each other means they are communicating. However, when it comes to personal relationships, your conversations have to be deep enough to form a strong connection. This starts with listening and doing your best to fulfill your partner's needs. Here are some specific tips on improving communication in relationships:

1. **Learn About Each Other's Communication Style** – Every individual has their preferred style of communicating. Some prefer to touch, others like talking while some use facial expressions and eye contact. You have to identify how your partner prefers to communicate and acknowledge it. Use their preferred style when communicating to them to build more trust and intimacy.
2. **Understand Your Partner's Needs** – We all have six fundamental needs, with the order of priority depending on the individual. They are certainty, variety, growth, significance, connection, and contribution. Identify the one that matters most to your partner and communicate with them in a way that satisfies that need.
3. **Avoid Emotions When Talking About Serious Issues** – Specific topics, such as money, children, and marriage, require a semblance of rationality. Such conversations don't end well when people are feeling angry or emotionally vulnerable. Try to minimize emotions when communicating about such serious issues.

4. **Learn to Compromise** – You don't have to win every argument even when you are right. The need to win an argument has ruined many relationships, and sometimes the best thing to do is give up ground to maintain a happy and respectful relationship.
5. **Add Humor to Your Communication** – This doesn't mean all your conversations should be peppered with jokes and pranks. You can, however, make a deliberate attempt to inject some playfulness and fun into your interactions to lighten the frustrations of everyday life.
6. **Keep in Touch Regularly** – Apart from verbal communication, couples can communicate via social media, email, or text. You can use technology to stay in touch or even communicate certain issues that you aren't confident speaking about face-to-face.
7. **Focus on the Current Issue** – Couples tend to bring up past conflicts whenever an argument arises rather than focus on the current topic. This adds confusion and past pain into the conversation, making it difficult to resolve the current issue. Stay present and focus on one issue until you find a solution.
8. **Get Professional Help** – Sometimes, it's best to consult a therapist if a couple cannot respect

each other during a conflict. If you've done everything you can and your partner still hasn't changed, family therapy or couples counseling may be an option.

MODELS OF COMMUNICATION

A model of communication is a graphical representation that helps explain the stages and processes of communication. These models are designed to help you enhance your skills and ability to communicate effectively. Though there has been extensive research conducted on this field, no single model has found general acceptance. However, there are five widely recognized models of communication:

Aristotle's Communication Model

This ancient model dates back to 300 BC. It describes how you can improve your communication skills and become an engaging and convincing communicator. Aristotle viewed communication from a rhetorical perspective, that is, speaking to an audience to persuade them. Since the flow of information is one-way, it is regarded as a linear model.

Aristotle's model focuses on five basic elements of communication: *the speaker, the speech, the occasion, the target audience, and the effect.* This model also focuses on other aspects such as ethos (your credibility), pathos (your ability to connect to the audience), and logos (the logic in your argument).

Shannon-Weaver Communication Model

This is probably the most globally accepted model and has been used to generate other models. Like Aristotle's model, it focuses on five elements: *the sender, the encoder, the channel, the decoder, and the receiver.* This model is radically different from Aristotle's model because it emphasizes the role of the encoder and decoder. The message must be encoded and decoded if it is to be understood in its proper context. It is also referred to as a transmission model of communication because it involves the transmission of information in the form of signals. As a result, it has been criticized as being more focused on engineering problems rather than facilitating human communication. This model also stresses the need to minimize any noise or errors in transmission through the repetition of messages. It also ignores feedback, which is a key part of any communication process.

Osgood Communication Model

In this model, there doesn't seem to be a difference between the sender and receiver. In other words, it is assumed that they are both encoding and decoding messages at the same time. For example, when engaging in instant messaging or a face-to-face chat, you and the other person are both encoding and decoding feedback in real-time. This is a two-way model that focuses on the social aspect of communication. Thus, it is usually applied in interpersonal communication where both the sender and receiver are physically present.

This model also relies heavily on the element of feedback provided through lively exchanges, for example, through asking and answering questions. This is considered a necessary way of understanding concepts and, therefore, the sender needs to provide good feedback. If it's a classroom situation where the students need to understand a difficult concept, the teacher must keep elaborating to ensure that they get the message.

Schramm Communication Model

This model takes into account the shared experiences of the sender and receiver. It focuses on the fact that they share information relevant to their common experiences, thus making their communication more effective. For example, two plumbers can communicate effectively because they perform the same job and probably share a similar background. Therefore, the sender and receiver can encode and decode information based on their experiences. But when the communication is between two people without shared experiences, perhaps a lawyer and a plumber, it is likely to be ineffective.

Newcomb's Communication Model

Unlike the others, Newcomb designed his model to explain the role of communication in social relationships. The model perceives the communication process as a significant part of maintaining social equilibrium. All communication between individuals is based on their social environment, and when their societal needs increase, they communicate to generate awareness and find solutions to their problems. This model shows the importance of creating effective communication mechanisms within a social environment to ensure that individuals work together to achieve a common desired outcome.

UNDERSTANDING YOUR AUDIENCE

So far, you have learned how to communicate with individuals. However, one-on-one conversations are very different experiences compared to communicating with an audience. Here are some tips on how to communicate effectively with small and large groups of people. These tips can be used for office presentations, speeches, podcasts, marketing emails, and blogs.

Read Your Audience

To get a good reading of the audience, you must know how to listen and ask questions. Use social media to communicate to your target demographic and get their thoughts and opinions. Study this treasure trove of information to identify what your audience needs, then give it to them.

Use Power Language

You need to make sure that your presentation's introduction has a powerful statement that locks in the audience's attention. Sprinkle your content with powerful and descriptive words that compel the audience to sit up, take action, or have an emotional response. You can use fear words (e.g., *agony, pitfall, and plummet*), encouragement words (e.g., *miracle, jubilant,* and *breathtaking*), lust words (e.g., *captivating, divine,* and *shameless*), anger words (e.g., *backstabbing, payback,* and *revolting*) and greed words (e.g., *jackpot, bonanza,* and *hurry*).

Focus on Diversity

Audience members may have diverse tastes when it comes to how they consume their content. Therefore, if you have a message, deliver it using a variety of channels to reach as many people in your target audience as possible. You can use Facebook videos, Instagram, LinkedIn posts, podcasts, etc. Remember to first do your research to identify which channels best fit your ideal audience.

Customize Your Communication

When you are speaking to an audience, you want them to stay engaged. You stand a better chance of achieving this if you understand what your audience cares about. You may need to change the way you present your message depending on their preferences. When planning a presentation, always consider the information that is most likely to impact them, then use appropriate stories and visual aids to make your message more relatable.

Becoming an effective communicator is the best way to ensure that you get your message across to people. Once you know the communication barriers to overcome and the right guidelines to follow, you can reach any audience, whether it's an individual or a group. Learning this skill then allows you to focus on putting your heart and soul into your message.

4

PUT YOUR HEART AND PASSION INTO IT

The main aim of communication is to get your message across clearly and effectively. There are many ways to achieve this goal. However, one skill that can make you more proficient in your communication is a can-do attitude. In this chapter, you will discover how to develop this skill as well as cultivate an enthusiastic and passionate communication style.

THE CAN-DO ATTITUDE

You probably know someone who is always positive about everything they do and say. They take challenges head-on, believing that they have what it takes to get things done. As a result, they seem to have a firm grip on their life, and no matter what obstacle they face, they always find a way to overcome it. This represents the can-do attitude – a mental level of confidence in your ability to achieve goals and create the life you want.

But why is it so important to develop a can-do attitude?

Let's answer this by looking at the opposite end of the spectrum. Have you ever met someone who doesn't believe that they can do anything? Every time you give them an idea or solution, they claim that they can't do it. They tend to dampen the mood and are always talking about negative things. It seems like they don't have a grip on their life, and due to their negativity, they run around trying to put out one fire after another in their life. This type of person isn't confident in their ability to tackle challenges and, therefore, fails to achieve much success in life.

Spending time with such negative people can bring you down because negativity is contagious. However, what's worse than spending time with negative people is having a negative attitude yourself. A can-do attitude is important because it shifts your mindset from weakness and victimhood to strength and success. When you believe that you have what it takes to succeed, you are more likely to put more energy into achieving your goals. A positive attitude empowers you to manifest your dreams and become the person you want to be.

Adopting this mindset is a choice that will change the way you view and interact with the world around you. You've probably had thousands of conversations with people throughout your life. Some were mundane and negative while others were filled with joy and exuberance. Of the two, which type did you enjoy most? Which kind of conversation stuck longer in your memory? It should be obvious that communicating positively with others helps not just to deliver the message but also to connect on a deeper level. A can-do attitude is contagious and can inspire others to strive for success in their own lives. When you feed others with positivity, they can also reciprocate by helping you manifest your dreams.

Apart from your communication with others, a can-do attitude also affects how you talk to yourself. Positive self-talk is a powerful way to motivate yourself because nobody knows you as you do. When life gets hard, you sit down and have a heart-to-heart conversation with yourself. You go straight to the source of the problem, which is your mind, and come up with a plan to make things work in your favor. This is a much better approach than shrugging your shoulders, giving up, or looking for someone to blame.

Living with a negative attitude can taint your perspective of life and significantly lower your chances of success. You are more likely to develop a passive personality, and your lack of assertiveness may cause others to dominate and take advantage of you. You may end up blaming others and think that you're always attracting bad things. But the truth is that your attitude has caused you to let go of the reins of your life.

If you are struggling to achieve your goals, you need to shift from an "I can't do it" to an "I can do it" mindset. This doesn't mean that you should embrace blind positivity and unrealistic optimism. You still have to be conscious of certain limitations in life. However, a can-do mindset spurs you to keep trying, hoping, and believing until you succeed.

HOW TO DEVELOP A CAN-DO ATTITUDE

If you want to shift your attitude from negative to positive, there are some powerful strategies that you can implement. Here are some practical ideas:

Develop a Growth Mindset

A growth mindset means you are always seeking to learn and do better. With a growth mindset, you automatically develop a can-do attitude because you understand that the power to succeed comes from your ability to acquire useful information. When you encounter a tough situation, you should try to find out more about the problem and how to deal with it. You can study books, check online resources, or talk to someone with more experience in that area. When you face a setback, understand that failure is not the end of the world. With a growth mindset, every failure is a learning opportunity and a chance to create a different path to success. You will increase your self-awareness and gain the confidence to chase after goals that others think are impossible.

Create Accountability

A can-do attitude requires you to push yourself past hurdles and excuses even when things get difficult. This becomes easier when you have people you love and trust to encourage you along the way. You can use accountability partners to motivate and inspire you to achieve your goals, especially when you're just starting to shift into a positive mindset.

Start by making a list of all the things you've achieved so far. A can-do attitude involves your emotions as much as your thoughts, so start by triggering some positive feelings about yourself. It doesn't matter if the list is a short one. The aim is to see what you've accomplished in the past and feel proud of yourself. The next step is to write a list of the goals to accomplish and share it with family, friends, and colleagues you trust. If you need extra motivation, share it with your social media followers. Tell them what your plans are and the timeframe for each goal. You will have a lot of people holding you accountable, and this will motivate you to follow through on your commitments. Finally, take small steps every day to achieve those goals and share the results with your accountability partners.

Align Your Thoughts, Feelings, and Actions

There is a prevailing notion in society that you can change your life by simply changing the way you think. Some say that all you need to do is change your emotions. Some argue that the most important thing is to make different choices, i.e., change your actions. However, research suggests that these models of change may be incomplete. According to Dr. Brene Brown, a social scientist and research professor at the University of Houston, real transformation only happens when there's congruency between all three. You have to bring your thoughts, emotions as well as actions into alignment.

Think of it this way: If you think positively all day but still feel negative, will you act positively or negatively? There is great power in positive thinking, but it's only one aspect of the whole. If you want to create a strong can-do mindset, you need to strengthen all three elements.

The first step you should take is to align your thoughts with your preferred actions. If you want to be more confident and speak more assertively, use positive affirmations to change the way you think. Tell yourself what you can do and what your strengths are. The change in thinking will change your biochemistry, causing you to walk and communicate with a more confident posture.

Once you start seeing small successes in your life, your emotions will quickly align with your actions. Positive results lead to positive feelings, and you will start feeling better about yourself. These positive emotions will then cycle back and support your positive mindset, thus reinforcing your can-do attitude.

Avoid Self-criticism

Negative self-talk is one of the main reasons why people develop low self-esteem. The more you tell yourself that you cannot do something, the less likely you are to do it. Stop being so self-critical whenever you fail at something. Identify your limiting beliefs and replace them with positive affirmations. Take a more positive look at your setbacks so that you can learn quickly and move forward.

Take Action on Your Ideas

A can-do attitude implies that you "can take action". In other words, you must do something. If you focus on executing your ideas instead of merely dreaming about them, you will generate enough momentum to push you forward. It doesn't matter how small the action is or how many times you fail at it in the beginning. At some point, you are going to learn enough to do it well. These small successes will motivate you to tackle bigger challenges.

Have Fun and Be Enthusiastic about Life

Life can get serious, so take some time to chill out and have some fun. Start seeing situations more as challenges and opportunities rather than unsolvable problems. Remember that life is an adventure, so develop an enthusiasm for life with all that it brings. Take the good with the not-so-good and keep reaching for your goals.

DEVELOPING ENTHUSIASM IN COMMUNICATION

The business world has always been synonymous with ideals such as stoic leadership, strong work ethic, good communication skills, and taking responsibility. Though these are necessary soft skills, it would serve you well to also develop traits such as passion and enthusiasm. These are two traits that come in handy, especially when communicating with others.

But why is enthusiasm so important when communicating with others?

Enthusiasm is an essential component of any successful speech. When you project enthusiasm to your audience, you are transformed from a mundane and forgettable speaker into a captivating and memorable communicator.

Think about this for a moment. Would you rather listen to a speech by an acclaimed expert who drones on and on in a low, monotonous tone or a less qualified individual who radiates passion and enthusiasm for the topic? It's difficult for an audience to pay attention to a message being delivered by someone who isn't eager to talk about the subject. By adding enthusiasm to your communication, you motivate the audience to want to listen to what you're talking about.

It is your passion and enthusiasm that attracts the audience to whatever you're communicating. It keeps them connected rather than drifting off, which is something that happens quite easily in a world filled with mindless distractions. They will wonder what it is about the topic that makes you so exuberant, and the only way they can find out is by staying engrossed in the message.

Enthusiasm shows that you are well-prepared. A good audience appreciates a speaker who has taken the time to prepare their message. You cannot expect to stand before an audience and speak from the top of your head without preparation. Enthusiasm is the product of a deep engagement with your message and conveying it with enough conviction to convince the audience that you are worth listening to.

Enthusiasm also shows that you are ready to invest energy into your speech. You cannot talk to an audience the same way that you address friends during a regular conversation. You must put more energy into your delivery if you want to get people's attention. Playing it safe may cost you the audience, and your message may never achieve its goal.

Imagine listening to Martin Luther King Jr. as he delivered his "I Have a Dream" speech at the Lincoln Memorial in Washington, D.C., on August 28, 1963. The level of passion and conviction in that speech is the reason why it's one of the most memorable speeches of all time. His speech ultimately spurred monumental social changes in America. Think about tuning in to the radio on June 4, 1940, as Winston Churchill urged his countrymen to defend their nation against the Nazis. The energy reverberating from his voice gave millions of Britons the courage to die for their homeland.

Of course, these are two examples of the greatest orators in history. Nobody is expecting you to suddenly communicate as they did. However, you can borrow a page from their book of communication skills. It may feel strange at first, especially if you're not used to communicating with such energy and enthusiasm. But with more practice, you will improve over time.

HOW TO DISPLAY ENTHUSIASM WHEN COMMUNICATING

Displaying enthusiasm is a great way to show your interest and passion for something. For example, if you are searching for a job, your resume should communicate your enthusiasm for that position to your potential employer. Your written words should create the impression of a person who knows what they want and is eager to get it. When you get to the interview, your speech and body language should reflect the energy and drive that you would bring into that organization. The same applies if you are on a date or meeting someone for the first time. People want to see that you are excited to be talking to them, and this increases the likelihood of your personal or professional success.

Use the following tips to help you communicate enthusiasm either in your writing or speech:

- **Use action verbs and power language** – Action verbs show people that you are excited about something. Power words help you add energy to whatever you're saying and grab people's attention. Instead of saying, "I like selling and want to help customers," you should say, "I am passionate about sales and determined to create an ideal experience for customers."
- **Use active speech** – The active voice conveys more energy and enthusiasm than the passive voice. Instead of saying, "My boss gave me a paid vacation after I closed that deal," you should say "I earned a paid vacation after closing that deal."
- **Love the topic** – The audience should feel your intense love for whatever you're talking about. If you don't believe in your message, the audience will pick up on it and see you as dishonest. To show enthusiasm for a topic, you should prepare and understand it well.
- **Use bullet points and subheadings** – This applies when communicating through your writing, whether it's a resume, blog, or book. Large chunks of text that go on page after page

are not just tiring to the eyes. It also shows the reader that you don't care enough to make the text easier for them to read.

With research showing that about 65% of communication is non-verbal, you need to learn how to display enthusiasm without using words. Here are some tips for communicating enthusiasm using body language:

- **Take up space** – If you are on stage, move around the podium rather than standing in one place. This allows the audience to feel engaged. If you're having a conversation while seated, keep your arms away from your body and avoid slouching in your chair.
- **Check your posture** – When you stand tall while speaking, you show the audience that you're confident in yourself and that whatever you're communicating must be important. It is also a display of a strong, energetic person.
- **Don't look at your watch** – Checking your watch during a conversation is a sign that you aren't fully engaged and would rather be somewhere else.
- **Use hand motions** – An enthusiastic person tends to use a lot of hand movements to demonstrate or highlight what they are saying.

Avoid crossing your arms or placing them on your hips for too long as it may make you appear disinterested.

- **Use facial expressions** – Facial expressions, such as smiling, nodding, or tilting your head, show that you're actively engaged and listening to what someone is saying. Smiling shows that you're excited about the conversation, and nodding is a good way to acknowledge what a person is saying or feeling.
- **Make eye contact** – When communicating, eye contact is important to establish a connection with an individual or group. However, be careful to not come across as creepy.
- **Dress for the occasion** – Whether it's a date, job interview, or a presentation, you should dress appropriately for that specific occasion. This shows that you consciously took the time to prepare and are ready for the role you're supposed to play.

Don't try to fake your passion and enthusiasm. You don't have to wave your arms around and shout at the audience to show your enthusiasm. It will be evident to all that you are simply being melodramatic. Let it come from deep within you through adequate preparation and the right amount of energy.

REFRAMING YOUR PROBLEMS

Negative things happen from time to time, no matter who you are or how hard you try to avoid them. Once you understand this, the important thing is to respond to negative situations in a way that is solution-driven rather than problem-focused. One of the techniques you can use to deal with negativity and problems is known as *reframing*.

Reframing is a cognitive coping strategy useful when dealing with a negative situation. It involves changing the way you think and feel about a difficult situation so that you get something positive out of it. When something negative happens, we often choose to attach meaning to the situation. The meaning you attach to it is the frame you give it. However, you have the power to change that frame so that you can feel differently about the situation.

Reframing should not be confused as a form of analysis where you ask yourself why the problem is happening. It is also not about finding the underlying problem. Reframing is about asking the right questions. You have to ask yourself whether the problem you are facing is the right problem to solve.

IMPORTANCE OF REFRAMING

Reframing is a positive coping mechanism that helps you manage stress. Negative events usually take you by surprise and end up affecting your emotions. For example, you may have a problem with your teenage daughter. She may be too headstrong, opinionated, or disrespectful by refusing to accept your house rules. If you perceive the situation negatively for too long, you will end up angry and stressed. But if you take the seemingly bad situation and find something good in it, you will avoid being sucked into a vortex of negative emotion. Since your teenager is strong-willed, she won't be a pushover when she goes out into the world. She will be an independent thinker rather than a lackey who accepts everything she is told.

In the business world, reframing is also used to promote creativity and innovation in problem-solving. When a problem arises within an organization, there is a tendency to try solving it using the same old methods that worked in the past. However, these old strategies may not be the best way to handle the issue. For example, café customers are complaining that the servers are too slow handling their orders. How would you solve the problem? The natural solution would be to hire more servers or train them to be faster. However, after reframing the question, the manager may decide to make the customers' wait time more pleasant. They can provide some entertainment to keep customers engaged as they wait for their orders.

As an aspect of emotional intelligence, reframing helps senior executives and managers control their feelings and those of their subordinates so that they can implement meaningful change. Problems can be opportunities in disguise, but you will never know this by seeing problems the same way you always have. Getting angry and apportioning blame may be the *modus operandi*, but it doesn't help solve anything. An organization may be having problems because it has refused to change with the times. By using the power of reframing, senior leadership may finally identify these difficulties as an opportunity to execute valuable changes in the workplace.

Reframing is also beneficial because it helps you learn lessons and shows you how to make better decisions. You are not going to learn anything new by looking at a difficult situation through the same lens as you always have. When you are stuck with a recurring problem, you may be tempted to believe that there's something that you're not seeing. You try looking at the problem more keenly, but you are still using the same lens as before. The real problem may be *the way* you're looking at the situation. By changing the frame you are looking through, you can learn something new and make a decision that finally solves the problem.

HOW TO REFRAME PROBLEMS

In business, reframing a problem enables you to see it as an opportunity to innovate and come up with novel solutions. But how do you reframe a problem? Here are five strategies that you can use:

Rethink the Question

When a problem arises, you tend to ask yourself a question that is supposed to help you come up with some workable solutions. Sometimes, you sit down with a group of other concerned people and brainstorm. However, before you begin the brainstorming process, you should first "frame-storm". This is a term coined by Stanford University's Tina Seelig, and it involves questioning the question that you're asking. You ask the group to first consider whether the question you're asking is the best question possible.

For example, if you're planning a company retreat, you would ask, "How do we make this day special for the team?" You would generate a set of ideas that would potentially solve the problem. However, if you reframe the question as, "How do we make this a memorable day for the team?", you could end up with a different set of solutions.

When you refocus the question, it changes the way you see the problem. "Special day" may mean doing something that costs a lot of money, but a "memorable day" may be simple and affordable. After you have reframed the question, you can then choose the best solution from the new ideas generated.

Consider the Bad Ideas

When you are thinking about a problem, you often feel the pressure to come up with really good ideas. Anything that appears ridiculous is usually tossed away. However, you should challenge yourself to re-evaluate those bad ideas as a way of coming up with non-obvious solutions. An idea that may seem terrible at first may provide a unique and wonderful perspective. Take all the bad ideas that you have generated and brainstorm on how to transform them into good ideas.

Challenge Your Assumptions

We usually have deeply ingrained assumptions about the way we should think or act. This is especially evident in large organizations where employees believe that things must be done in a specific way according to industry norms. But if you are facing a challenge within the industry, consider unpacking some of your assumptions. By challenging some of the rules, you may generate ideas that solve the problem and change the way the industry operates. To do this, you can make a list of all the assumptions you have and then consider what would happen if you went against them.

Break Down the Challenge into Smaller Ones

If you're facing a big and complex challenge, you may find it difficult to solve as it is. However, you can reframe the challenge into several smaller ones, then solve each challenge independently. This way, you can quickly come up with small solutions that can be implemented immediately. Some of these minor solutions may not even need permission from senior management which can sometimes delay the process. These small improvements can generate the momentum needed to open up new possibilities.

Reach Out to More People

When seeking advice on how to reframe a question, you are likely to go to the same people who have helped you in the past. You're also likely to consult only those individuals who are concerned with the issue. However, as part of the reframing process, you should consult other departments not affected by the problem. Talk to customers and other stakeholders and ask them how they would reframe the question.

Success is a mental game, whether it's in your business, career, or personal life. A can-do attitude will shift your mindset to one of growth and progress. There is also hidden value to be found in difficult situations. Reframing is an effective way of changing your mindset and achieving a positive outcome at the same time. It is powerful because it forces you to challenge conventional thinking and find an innovative and creative solution.

In a world that is becoming increasingly chaotic and complex, it is important to learn how to change the way you perceive things that appear as negative. By learning to make lemonade out of lemons, you may discover that lemonade is exactly what you needed all along.

5

SELF-MOTIVATION AND INSPIRING OTHERS

Self-awareness plays a major role in how you step up to the world around you. When you know and understand yourself, you make decisions that help you achieve your goals faster and more effectively. Dig deep and find a source of motivation within you that does not exist anywhere else. This inner power can help you achieve your success in a way that inspires others to achieve their greatness. In this chapter, you will discover how to find a personal source of motivation and learn how to inspire others to do the same.

SELF-MOTIVATION

Let's start by asking a few questions:

- Why do you get out of bed every morning to go to work or school?
- Why do you run your business?
- What motivates you in life?

Here's a candid truth. Most people are motivated by the wrong things. Some are motivated by a sense of obligation. They wake up and go to work just to pay their bills. Others feel obligated to please their parents and peers, so they stay in jobs they hate or take a college course that doesn't resonate with them. Of course, there's nothing wrong with having obligations. Your obligations are often strong enough to get you to do things you normally wouldn't want to. But feeling obligated is not the same thing as being motivated. At the same time, being motivated by others is not as powerful as self-motivation.

But why is self-motivation important?

Without a doubt, the greatest form of motivation you can develop is self-motivation. Self-motivation can be defined as a force that drives you to work toward your goals so you can grow and achieve personal fulfillment. When you are self-motivated, your drive comes from within rather than from outside sources.

Let's say you're running a business. You spend your days feeling that being an entrepreneur is something you have to do to provide for your family and keep them happy. You have the external signs of success but are largely unfulfilled. You don't have a passion for your work, and you often feel drained of energy, especially when things don't go according to plan.

Now let's explore a second scenario. You are running a business that you're enthusiastic about and love to do. You are comfortable with yourself and don't need an external push to work on your business. You take on whatever challenges and tasks come your way, and are excited to spend time and energy accomplishing your goals.

Which of these two scenarios would you rather be in? It would be the second scenario, wouldn't it? When you do something because you genuinely want to, you are more likely to find success, fulfillment, and joy. But when you do something out of obligation or to please others, you won't find much satisfaction or success.

IMPORTANCE OF SELF-MOTIVATION

Self-motivation is important for several reasons. The first is that it helps you cope better with stress. Even when a task becomes challenging, it is possible to stay focused and find a solution despite the tough conditions. You are simply happy to be engaged in your work regardless of how stressful things get.

Self-motivation is also effective because it is driven by an inner desire to achieve a goal and the inherent rewards that come with it. Life becomes more satisfying when you are self-motivated because you experience such tremendous personal growth that then generates more success. A person who has to be pushed and prodded to do something may end up completing the task, but they won't experience the satisfaction that comes with learning and growing.

Look at the lives of some of the most accomplished inventors, innovators, athletes, and artists throughout history. Some of these men and women were considered crazy because they appeared to be chasing goals that were way beyond them. But they kept moving forward because they didn't need the outside world to motivate them. They were engaged in labors of love that invoked enough passion to motivate them to excel in their field. Today, we not only reap the fruits of their efforts but are also inspired to walk in their footsteps.

Your self-motivation also shows in the way you carry yourself and communicate with others. Being self-motivated shows that you love what you do, and this attitude inspires others to also seek their inner motivations. You create a positive vibe around you that makes others feel that they too have permission to seek fulfillment and a deeper meaning to their lives.

SELF-MOTIVATION AND EMOTIONAL INTELLIGENCE

In Chapter 2, you learned about emotional intelligence and the role it plays in your communication. You learned that emotional intelligence has four key attributes – self-management, self-awareness, social awareness, and relationship management. As it turns out, self-motivation is also a major component of emotional intelligence and is linked to all four attributes. Let's explore this connection further.

It's very difficult to be self-motivated if you are lacking in self-management skills. Highly motivated people can manage their thoughts and emotions well enough to develop the discipline to reach their goals. Once they commit to a task, they stay in control of their emotions and keep working until they succeed. The same applies to self-awareness. The more aware you are of your emotions, strengths, and weaknesses, the easier it is for you to discover your inner source of motivation.

No man is an island. You live in a world populated by people with different personalities and value systems. Some will be of great help while others will do their best to be a great hindrance. No matter how self-motivated you may be, it is extremely useful to also develop social awareness and relationship management. You need to learn how to be empathetic and relate well with others, especially when there is tension in the relationship.

What use would it be to be self-motivated if your lack of empathy is constantly causing conflicts in your workplace? Your aggressive communication style may rub so many people the wrong way that nobody would be willing to team up with you. Alternatively, you could be so passive that family members are always burdening you with their mundane tasks, yet you don't dare to refuse. Yes, you may be self-motivated, but you'll spend more time working for others' interests instead of your own.

Self-motivation is extremely relevant to emotional intelligence as it highlights your ability to understand yourself, relate to others and successfully achieve your goals. Therefore, self-motivation can be broken down into four elements:

- Achievement – A need to meet certain goals and standards
- Commitment – Sticking to your goals and desires

- Initiative – Being prepared to act on opportunities
- Optimism – Looking ahead and embodying a can-do attitude

The bottom line is that you need to understand how your emotional intelligence feeds into your self-motivation. You can increase your odds of success when you align these two factors together.

HOW TO DEVELOP MOTIVATION IN THE WORKPLACE

We all go through periods when we feel stuck in some kind of a motivational slump. When this happens, you have to be armed with techniques and strategies that can get you out of that negative cycle. Here are some steps to help you develop your motivation:

Know Your Values

It is important to do work that is connected to your values. For example, if you value growth and transformation, find work that promotes continual learning. If you value contribution, make sure that your work helps improve the lives of others. Your values will keep you motivated even on days when you don't feel as enthusiastic as you should. You can also find a meaningful metaphor to attach to your values. For example, when engaging in a project, don't see yourself as simply doing a task. Tell yourself that you're mastering your craft. Try to find a useful metaphor that can fuel your desire to succeed.

Find Motivated Peers

It is easier to stay motivated when you are surrounded by people who are passionate about their work. Try to spend more time around those who are motivated and positive. Reach out to a co-worker who likes sharing ideas or a friend who sees opportunities in everything. As you do this, avoid negative people as much as possible especially when you are feeling unmotivated. Misery loves company.

Find Your "Why"

What is it that compels you to follow a particular path? That compelling purpose is your *'why"*, and it can be a powerful motivator to help you get back on track when things get difficult. If you realize that your *why* is weak or doesn't align with your values, don't be afraid to change it.

Keep Learning

When you try to learn as much as you can about the work you are interested in, you become more competent at it. This competence breeds confidence, and your self-confidence feeds your inner desire to achieve your goals. The more you learn, the easier it becomes to start new projects because you already know what to do to get the job done.

Shift Your Focus

There are times when you are faced with a huge project but lack the motivation to even get started. You know what to do and how to do it, but you cannot muster the enthusiasm to begin. The problem could be that you are overthinking. Your worry may have frozen you in your tracks, and you can't generate enough momentum to get the project off the ground. If this is the case, try focusing on something else, such as a smaller task that's easier to accomplish. When you succeed in that trivial task, use the momentum you've generated to motivate you to begin the big project.

Track Your Progress

Research shows that your mind tends to focus more on negative things than it does on the positive. This negative bias occurs because the brain is built to have greater sensitivity to negative stimuli than positive or neutral ones. But what does this have to do with motivation?

One of the reasons why you feel unmotivated is your focus on past losses. When you focus on all the negative things that you've been through, you may lose the drive to go after your goals. The solution is to always keep track of your successes so that you have a reference point to motivate you in the future. Monitor the progress of your projects and record any wins along the way. You should also celebrate your successes whenever possible to create memories of the success you've achieved and the rewards.

Change Your Feelings

One of the fastest ways to motivate yourself is to recall the feelings you had when things were good. Sit down and visualize what it felt like when you accomplished a past work project. Remember the emotions of fulfillment, joy, and excitement you had, then use these positive emotions to elevate your motivation. Another technique is to associate your work with a positive feeling. For example, if you're engaging in work that seems dull, play your favorite song so that it masks the drudgery of the task.

Impress Yourself First

Most people tend to do things as a way to impress others. The problem with this approach is that if those people are not impressed by your work, you're not going to feel motivated to keep going. Therefore, to generate that internal drive to accomplish a goal, you should focus on impressing yourself first. Set high standards for your work, then meet them. Connect to your inner passion and set the bar for yourself rather than letting others set the bar for you.

Reframe Your Language

Words have the power to affect your emotions and attitude. By changing the way you speak, you can alter your mood and attitude. For example, instead of telling yourself that you "have to do" something, say "I choose to do it." Change the way you speak and adopt a motivating language that works in your favor.

Help Others

Helping others stay motivated enables them to succeed in achieving their goals. This in turn will also motivate you to succeed in your endeavors. For example, you can start by sharing information about effective communication skills with co-workers. If you have a blog, share stories about your success with your subscribers and ask them to share theirs. You may be pleasantly surprised at just how motivating it can be to read other people's success stories.

Motivation Techniques

When it comes to developing self-motivation, there are tons of activities, exercises, and even meditations that can help you get started. There are quick and easy things you can do, but there are also some more intense techniques available.

Here is a list of some simple activities for quick motivation:

1. Listen to some motivational music, such as "Can't Hold Us" by Macklemore and Ryan Lewis, "Don't Stop Believing" by Journey, or "It's My Life" by Bon Jovi.
2. Watch a motivational movie. Some good examples include "The Pursuit of Happyness", "Of Mice and Men", and "Rain Man".
3. Read a book written by a motivational author, such as Tony Robbins, Jim Rohn, or Napoleon Hill.

If you want to go deeper, here is a list of more powerful motivational techniques:

1. Choose deeply personal goals. When you set goals that you are closely connected to, it is easier to get excited about them. Your enthusiasm will drive you to work toward those goals.

2. Celebrate whenever you achieve a goal or take a step toward a major one. It's easy to get caught up in the everyday chase to reach your goals and forget to take time to reward yourself for the work you've already accomplished. Also, if you have a big goal that seems intimidating, reward yourself after you take a couple of steps toward it. This will motivate you to maintain your progress.
3. Use visualization to see yourself crossing the finish line. Visualization is a powerful tool for motivation because it allows you to glimpse the future. If you're feeling unmotivated when working on a project, visualize yourself achieving your goal, and feel the satisfaction that comes with that accomplishment. Channel that positive emotion into the present and use it to spur you forward. Another related technique would be to visualize what it would feel like *not* to reach your goals. This negative emotion may also be powerful enough to motivate you.
4. Create a vision board and place it where you can see it often. A vision board is a collection of images that represent your dreams, goals, and aspirations. When you regularly look at these visual representations, you feel inspired to make them a reality. You can download any

image from the internet, as long as it's relevant to your goal, and post it on your board.
5. Don't ignore your physiological needs. We tend to overlook our lower-level needs when we are chasing a big goal. How many times have you skipped lunch or stayed up late for weeks just to finish an important project? This may be effective at first, but it can also drain you of the very energy you need to achieve your goals. Some people go even as far as ignoring their personal safety to accomplish a task. It's important to find a balance where you pay attention to your physiological needs so that you can stay motivated in the long term.
6. Use Neuro-linguistic Programming (NLP) to change the way you think and act. NLP is a set of tools and skills that reveal the type of communication most important to you. Through NLP, you can discover which of your senses is more highly valued and influences your communication the most. Once you understand your preferred communication mode (auditory, visual, kinesthetic, etc.), you can use that awareness to find the best way to motivate yourself. For example, if you are auditory, you can use motivational music. If

you are kinesthetic, you can hit the gym to fire you up for the task ahead.
7. Find an accountability partner. Look for someone who can hold you accountable in case you fail to meet your goal. By committing to someone else, you make it harder to change your plans or quit prematurely.

MEDITATIONS FOR BOOSTING MOTIVATION

Apart from the activities that can motivate you, there are also specific types of meditation techniques that are effective. Try this guided meditation and see how it works for you.

1. Close your eyes.
2. Take a deep breath through your nose until you expand your lungs. Slowly breathe out through your mouth. Feel yourself relaxing with every inhalation.
3. Inhale again and feel the air as it fills your lungs. Hold your breath for a count of two, then release the air through your mouth. You will begin to feel peaceful as you focus on your breathing.
4. Visualize yourself standing at the foot of a cliff.

Imagine a series of steps cut into the rock leading to the top of the cliff.

5. As you climb the steps, be aware of your emotions. With each step you ascend, let go of the tension in your body.
6. You can feel a strong positive sensation pulling you forward. This sensation gets stronger with each step you take.
7. When you get to the top, take a moment to focus on your breathing. Gently inhale and exhale. Let your breathing flow naturally. Order your muscles to relax to relieve any tension.
8. Imagine a wooden arch doorway in front of you. Reach out and feel the texture of the old wood. The door doesn't have a handle, but you sense an urge to go to the other side. You realize that the door can only open by using a word that's special to you. Take a moment to pick a password, then mentally say it.
9. The door opens to reveal a cavern with walls that glow with luminous green color. You hear water flowing. There's a peaceful sensation in the cavern, and you are not afraid.
10. You see a pool built into the rock, and the emerald-colored water shines.
11. Sit on the edge of the pool and look deeply

beyond your reflection. You see images of your past. They reveal the happiest times of your life when you achieved all that you wanted. Let all these memories play out as you recall how you felt motivated, confident, and energized at that time. Ask yourself why you felt so happy back then.

12. Picture yourself as an onlooker watching you sit by the pool. Get a sense of what you look like through the eyes of another. What does your body language reveal about you?
13. Let peaceful thoughts wash over you and realize that you have the power to do anything in life.
14. Move away from the pool but hold onto the happy memories you just saw.
15. As you walk through the cavern, see the morning daylight entering through the cracks in the walls. You feel the warm sunlight on your skin, and you become more content and relaxed. There is no tension or dissatisfaction, just pure peace and happiness.
16. As you walk further into the cavern, you see a waterfall. Sit on a large rock and watch the clear water splash on the rocks and flowers around the waterfall. You feel abundant and carefree, and you know you can achieve

whatever you want. Think of yourself as a unique and special person.
17. Visualize all the things you can do. Let the images be framed by the clear water. Ask yourself what you really want in life. What would make you truly content and confident?
18. See yourself reaching out and touching your dreams. You can achieve all your desires if you work on them.
19. Let the positive and powerful atmosphere fill your being. Feel confident and relaxed as you stare at the water.
20. Take your dreams with you as you walk out of the cavern. When outside, inhale deeply and allow yourself to be filled with self-motivation.
21. Open your eyes. You are now ready to accomplish your goals.

HOW TO INSPIRE OTHERS

Understanding and tapping into your inner source of motivation are incredibly powerful. However, you aren't doing all this just for personal gain. You can help and inspire others to also find the inspiration they need. This is especially true if you are an authentic leader who wants to excite others to partake in a shared vision. This can be at the workplace or within your family. But how do you use your motivation to influence and inspire other people? Here are 10 ways to do it:

Appeal to Their Emotions

There are two primary ways to motivate people. One is fear and one is love. Fear can be a powerful motivating force when you want to get people to perform a task. You can threaten them with loss or pain, and they will find the energy to get things done. However, this is not a good long-term plan. Fear saps people's energy, and they'll end up more demotivated than before. It's better to use more positive ways such as getting people excited about a goal or making them feel like a part of something greater than themselves.

Identify Each Person's Unique Motivators

One of the secrets to motivating people is to know how each one is motivated. This is important because what motivates one person may not necessarily motivate another. The best leaders understand the tendencies of each person they work with and how to bring out the best in everyone. This means that you have to spend time with them, listening and observing them keenly every time you interact. People feel more inspired when they think their leader genuinely has their best interests at heart. Therefore, learn how each individual is motivated, and then show them how the overall strategy relates to them.

Set Clear Goals

Intrinsic motivation comes from the setting of clear and specific goals. When you clearly state measurable goals, the tasks involved, and the deadline for completion, you are more likely to inspire greater output and team performance. This eliminates the chances for confusion or conflict. Once you have communicated a clear vision, there may be some who do not agree with it. Instead of trying to force them to conform, show them that your strategies are correct and will work.

Stick to Your Principles

To motivate people to perform better, you have to show them that you have the right principles. You cannot cut corners and do shoddy work, and yet expect the best from your team. If you want to portray a powerful role model, you must do the right things.

Challenge Them

If a goal is too easy, people become lazy. If the goal is too difficult, they may quit because they feel they cannot achieve it. You have to find a balance where the goal is neither too easy nor too intimidating. Make sure that the goal feels challenging enough to take on.

Establish a Motivating Environment

Everyone wants to work in an environment where they feel empowered to play their role according to their strengths. You can monitor your team's work but avoid being too controlling as this may reduce their motivation. You should also give people a chance to chip in with their ideas and involve them when making decisions. Instead of telling them to come to you when there's a problem, facilitate ways where they can collaborate to find solutions. The more confident and competent they become, the more motivated they will feel. As Vala Afshar said, people become a team not because they work together but because they care for, trust, and respect each other.

Don't Ask for Too Much

You can ask someone to work late for one or even a couple of nights but don't expect them to work late every day for an indefinite period. They will lose their motivation, become frustrated, and start to slack off. Set a clear end date so that they know that the situation is only temporary.

Sacrifice As Much As Everyone Else

When you ask people to work with you toward a shared vision, you should also be willing to spend as much time and energy working as they do. If they are working late or on weekends, so should you. Remember that people are always looking at your level of motivation to inspire them. Let your character and behavior inspire them to put in the effort required. After all, great leaders lead from the front and share the load.

Appreciate and Value People

If you want people to invest their time and energy working toward a goal, you have to appreciate and value them. Your team members need to feel that you are personally interested in them and recognize their unique input and effort. Show them the respect and admiration that they deserve. You should also consider rewarding your team as motivation to push harder to achieve the goal.

Enable Them Develop Their Skills

Most businesses put their employees through regular technical programs in the name of skill development. However, most of these programs are done merely to keep the business compliant. Instead, provide them with meaningful new skills that aren't necessarily part of their current roles. When your employees see that you value their overall growth, they will feel more inspired to improve their output.

Getting the most out of yourself and others is a very important skill. You can't always rely on external factors to motivate you. You must look for that inspiration within you. At first, you may be doing it for yourself, but you will realize that your self-motivated behavior influences those around you. The more success you achieve, the more likely it is that you will end up impacting more people. This will come in handy when negotiating with different people, especially those more powerful than you.

6

THE ART OF NEGOTIATING

At any given moment, you are exerting influence on the people around you. This may come through your words or body language, and you may not even be aware of it. Influence can either be positive or negative, and it may work for or against you. In this chapter, you will discover how to influence others, especially in the workplace. You will also discover how to negotiate effectively while still maintaining a sense of morality and ethics.

This is important because you don't want to blur the lines between influence and control. Contrary to what most people think, they are not the same thing. Influence is the ability to produce the desired outcome without getting attached to the result. You can influence your children by using incentives or consequences, but you should understand that how they respond is their choice. Control, on the other hand, is seeking to guarantee the desired outcome by any means necessary. It is trying to take away a person's right to choose their own path, and this often leads to resistance and frustration. Influence is more powerful than control, and therefore, you should seek to have the former rather than the latter.

HOW TO INFLUENCE OTHERS

Whether you are in a leadership position or not, you need to learn how to influence people. As mentioned before, you are already doing it to some degree, so you might as well learn how to do it intentionally for the greater good. There are three main ways of influencing people:

Logical Appeal

A logical appeal means influencing others by tapping into their intellectual and rational positions. By influencing their head, you are trying to get them to agree with the rationale behind your idea. You can achieve this by sharing facts from a recognized institution or appealing to their organizational belief system.

Emotional Appeal

An emotional appeal influences people's hearts by connecting with their emotions. You can achieve this by connecting your message or goal with a personal value. An emotional appeal usually relies on the values of the people you are trying to influence. Charity organizations do this extremely well when seeking donations or asking for volunteers.

Cooperative Appeal

Cooperative appeal involves consultation, collaboration, and team formation. You achieve this by reaching out to others, asking for their input, and encouraging them to work together. Whereas the first two ways involve appealing to the head and heart, this one involves appealing to the hands.

But how do you know which one of these three approaches to use when trying to influence people?

The simple answer is that you should select a strategy based on the situation you're facing. Some instances may require more of a head influence. A good example would be when trying to convince employees to work overtime to finish a project before senior executives from the head office arrive. Another factor that determines which appeal to use is the audience you're trying to influence. For example, an emotional appeal is more likely to work on women than men. Finally, you should consider your strength in each type of appeal. If you're not strong in a particular appeal, then consider combining two appeals as necessary.

AUTHENTICITY

If you're going to influence others, you have to rely on your unique skill set and character traits. In other words, you influence others by being authentic and congruent with your values, especially if you are in a leadership position. A true leader shows others the way by walking their talk. It's not just about telling people who you are and what you do. If you want to influence others through your authenticity, you have to lead by example.

You cannot ask your employees or team members to do something that you would not be willing to do yourself. If you ask them to do something against your core values, you will end up having a negative influence on others. Influence is only meaningful if it comes from a place of authenticity, which then gives you the credibility to continue to be a positive influence.

STRATEGIES FOR PROFESSIONAL INFLUENCE

If there is one place where you should consciously exert your influence, it is the workplace. Your workplace is an area where you need to cooperate with diverse people with varying interests to meet certain objectives. Therefore, it makes a lot of sense to build your capacity to influence colleagues so that you can tap into their knowledge and skills to achieve results. Furthermore, influencing others is one of the primary leadership skills required in every role in an organization. So, what do you need to do to influence others? Here are some key influencing skills:

Practice Organizational Intelligence

In every organization, you will find a specified formal structure that determines the power hierarchy and how different roles are linked within the organization. However, there is also an informal structure that is often not talked about. This usually represents how work *really* gets done. If you are seeking influence, you must recognize and understand both the formal and informal structure. This kind of organizational intelligence is akin to political savviness, and it is a mindset as well as a skill set. You may not particularly like politics, but it is a necessary part of every organization. You can use political savvy to push forward the goals of the organization productively and ethically.

Promote Yourself and the Team

Most people regard self-promotion as a negative thing. It may evoke an image of someone selfish, arrogant, and a braggart. However, self-promotion is more than just a tool for advancing your career. You can use it as a way to achieve objectives that are for the good of all. An influential leader should leverage self-promotion for the right reasons. Promoting yourself can also provide you with the right amount of visibility and opportunity to push forth great ideas that can benefit your team or organization. The success of these ideas will then generate more pride within the organization and improve cooperation.

Before you can effectively engage in self-promotion, there are two valuable skills you should learn. The first is to find ways of bringing an audience together. You can do this by asking more people to join your team or problem-solving initiative. The second skill is to find ways of stepping into the spotlight, especially during events and meetings. You should do this strategically without stepping on the toes of others.

Build and Maintain Trust

Trust is the glue that binds people together. It's often easy to build but hard to maintain. Without trust, you may be forced to rely on force and aggressive communication to get people to comply. However, you won't be able to get them to fully commit their energy and creativity or get everyone on the same page. Therefore, building trust is vital when collaborating to tackle challenges or making strategic shifts.

This doesn't mean you have to be soft all the time. The truth is that people are seeking leaders who can balance toughness with empathy. This is important during times of looming chaos when people look for leaders who understand and support them but who are also willing to lead them into uncharted waters. During times of transition, people have to be motivated to get out of their comfort zones. An influential leader should firmly and urgently guide others, yet patiently listen to their concerns. This balancing act may seem contradictory, but if you use it wisely and at the right times, you will foster and maintain trust.

Leverage Your Networks

To develop influence at the workplace, you need to recognize the importance of cultivating your networks. Organizations are constantly changing in size and shape. Therefore, your professional networks must also be dynamic, and you have to continually grow and strengthen them. Once you've created a strong network, don't waste favors by asking for useless things. You must learn how and when to leverage the power of your networks.

Listen and Respect Others' Opinions

The best way to get your colleagues to support you and your agenda is to listen to what they have to say. Give them your full attention so they feel heard. Make sure that your body is facing theirs and avoid things like reaching for your phone. This gives the impression that you would rather be somewhere else. When you make people feel heard, it shows them that you value their opinion.

However, disputes and conflicts of opinion are also common within the workplace. Sometimes, people just see things differently. Most people approach such situations with the mentality of right versus wrong. When you tell someone that their opinion is wrong, they become defensive and may not want to listen to anything else you have to say. This diminishes your influence.

A better approach would be to say, "I respect your opinion, but I have a different perspective." This is less offensive to their self-esteem, and they may be more willing to listen to the reasons why you hold a different opinion. By respecting their opinion, they keep an open mind, and this allows you to influence them.

Watch Your Body Language

Whenever you approach a person, they automatically question whether you are an ally or an enemy. This is part of our hardwiring and is tied to our survival instinct. This means that your level of influence is determined by how you come across to the other person even before you open your mouth. Therefore, your body language is critical to sending the message that you are a friend that can be trusted. You also want to come across as being assertive rather than subordinate or aggressive.

For example, if you're meeting an unfamiliar colleague, stand or sit up straight with your shoulders back. Slouching makes you appear subordinate and lacking authority. You should also keep your arms by your side rather than crossed. Maintain a lower tone than normal as this helps you sound more powerful and less anxious.

Become an Expert

Your professional influence is directly proportional to your level of competence. If people recognize you as an expert in your field, they instinctively pay attention to anything you have to say about your area of expertise. Developing your expertise takes time. However, you can start by attending relevant conferences, taking a class, or even writing articles online or for the company newsletter.

Be Strategic

Let's say you have an idea you would like to promote, but you need key decision-makers to buy into it. You can create a chart showing all the important decision-makers and the role they play. Ask yourself how you can influence each one directly or indirectly. Consider those who are likely to oppose you and how to turn them into allies. You should also consider when and how to approach them. This may seem like scheming to some, but it's an effective strategy to get people on your side.

Empower Others

You can impact people's lives by what you say or do. Unfortunately, those very same people may forget your words and deeds. However, one thing that people rarely forget is how you made them feel. When you motivate and empower people to succeed in the workplace, they will remember the positive feeling that you stirred within them. You will gain their respect and gratitude, and as a result, you will have a greater influence over them.

Be Assertive, Not Bossy

To successfully achieve a vision or complete a project, you need people to work together synergistically from start to finish. If you are the leader of such an initiative, you need to maintain a level of assertiveness to keep everyone performing at their best. However, you cannot afford to come across as needlessly aggressive or bossy. You cannot influence people by ordering them around or refusing to listen to their feedback. This will generate disquiet within your team, and people may refuse to perform as expected. Communicate your expectations clearly and coordinate with everyone involved to achieve your collective goals.

HOW TO DEVELOP NEGOTIATING SKILLS

One of the core aspects of being influential is your ability to negotiate. The word "negotiation" often evokes images of corporate mergers, political deals, and even hostage situations. However, negotiation is something we all do in our personal and professional lives. You've probably negotiated a contract with an employer or compromised on a family holiday destination. The point is that negotiating is something you are already doing, so why not learn some crucial skills while you're at it? Your negotiation skills determine how well you present yourself and your ideas, and whether you can convince people to help you reach your goals.

At the same time, some negotiation situations are not the same as others. For example, it's easier to negotiate with someone who is either your junior or peer compared to an individual who is more powerful than you. Negotiating with your boss or even a high-profile client requires that you have a higher negotiating skill level. In such cases, what do you do to improve your chances of success? Here are 10 tips to use when negotiating:

Be Confident

Some forms of negotiation can be nerve-wracking, especially if you are aware of the threat of competition. This is common when going for a job interview or trying to get a contract as a vendor. Most people become fearful and end up lowering their demands or requirements. You cannot negotiate well unless you are self-confident and recognize your uniqueness. There is a reason why you were called for that interview or shortlisted as a potential vendor. The other party must have recognized something unique that you can bring to the table. You need to examine the strengths and expertise that you have. Focus on the skills that you have that the other candidates do not. Your confidence will help you negotiate from a position of power and influence.

Understand Your Goals and Theirs

You should walk into every negotiation with a strategy including a list of objectives and your motivation for seeking those aims. This will remind you of what you are willing to accept and what would cause you to walk away. At the same time, you should also study the other person's goals, motivations, and obstacles. This way, you can present your goals as solutions to their problems rather than a list of demands.

Be Well-prepared

The most effective strategy for negotiation is to prepare well for it. You should have a brainstorming session before the meeting to devise creative solutions that will be tenable for all parties. Anticipate the potential arguments that the other party may have and come up with counter-demands. Let's say you are a vendor, and a client refuses to adjust their price point. You can propose that they offer you a longer contract that maintains their preferred price but assures you revenue for a longer timeframe.

You should also prepare by researching any information regarding their past patterns, so you're prepared to make your case. Let's say that a potential employer offers you a specific salary for a job, and you consider it to be too low. Thanks to your research, you could counter by telling them that other employees in the same role and with similar experience are earning much more. Your level of preparation will determine whether you fail or succeed in getting what you want.

Listen Well and Ask Questions

When you take the time to listen to the other person during a negotiation, you build trust and show them that you're interested in what they have to say. Asking questions keeps the other party on their toes and encourages them to defend their position. If they are unable to answer your questions, you may have just shifted power in your favor. For example, if your boss tells you that you're not the right fit for a particular executive position, ask them to describe the qualities of the ideal candidate. Once they answer the question, you could explain to them how you already have those traits or have the potential to develop them.

Avoid Reacting in Anger

If you are in a negotiation with a more powerful individual, you should expect some sort of power play. People in power sometimes exercise their authority by making threats or intimidating others. Therefore, you should avoid the tendency to react negatively or take things personally. Just because they say something in a negative tone or display bad behavior, it doesn't mean you should respond in the same way too. If you try to retaliate with a negative tone, you will lose. Keep the discussion focused on your goals and stick to your strategy.

Maintain Flexibility

If you want to be a great negotiator, be prepared with more than one strategy. Each strategy should provide you with extra room to maneuver in case one fails during the negotiation. This flexibility can be in many forms. You can ask the person you're negotiating with for some time to brainstorm solutions. You can also suggest that they tell you more about the rationale behind their argument. Flexibility allows you to find a position that works for you and also makes the other party feel like they've succeeded.

Use Coinage

Coinage is a valuable currency used in negotiation. It refers to something that has low value to you but high value to the other side. It is a small concession that you make to sweeten the deal for the other side, for example, offering a free warranty for a product you're selling. You can use it during the latter stages of a negotiation to enable you to get more of what you want.

Use Silence as a Tool

Talking too much can make you appear nervous and also prevents you from listening. During a negotiation, silence can project power and give you the chance to gain valuable information from the other party. Let's say you make an offer, and the person rejects it. Instead of jumping in immediately, stay silent for a few seconds. The other person will become uncomfortable and try to fill the silence by talking about why they rejected your offer. As they do this, they may reveal valuable information regarding their needs and motivations. When you finally speak, use this new information to your advantage.

Never Give Without Taking

Every negotiation involves making concessions. However, you should never make unilateral concessions where you give away something without getting anything in return. If you give without taking, the person may consider this a weakness and begin to make greater demands on you. Every concession you make must be accompanied by reciprocation.

Never Negotiate "Alone"

Even if you are negotiating for yourself and happen to be the ultimate decision-maker, don't let the other side know that. When they make an offer that leaves you feeling cornered, ask for some time to step outside the room to consult "your boss". Of course, you're only stepping outside to get some time to think. This helps to take the pressure off so that you avoid accepting a bad deal. If you have to reject the offer, tell the other side that it is the final decision-maker that has rejected the deal.

Be Willing to Walk Away

Don't depend too much on having a positive outcome in a negotiation. You have to be willing to walk away if you cannot get a deal that works for you. This doesn't mean that you should give in too quickly. If you enter the negotiation feeling desperate to make a deal, the other side will eat you alive. The other negotiator should sense that "no" is one of your options.

HOW TO GROW A WIN-WIN MINDSET

One of the traits that successful people have in common is their win-win mindset. In all their interactions, they try to make sure that the situation ends up being mutually beneficial to all involved. Win-win goes beyond competitiveness and exclusion of others. It is a more cooperative approach to life where people deal with each other respectfully and agree that there are enough resources for everyone. This is a great frame of mind and heart to have when negotiating because you focus more on principles rather than jostling for power and position. If you're interested in growing a win-win mindset, here are some tips that may help:

Maintain an Abundance Mindset

One of the major reasons why most people fight for a win-lose outcome is that they have a scarcity mindset. They believe that there are simply not enough resources, so they have to grab every opportunity at others' expense. But when you believe that the world is abundant and there's enough for everyone, you are no longer afraid of losing. You no longer have to destroy the competition or deny others the chance to also succeed. With an abundance mindset, it becomes easier to negotiate a mutually satisfying outcome.

Integrate the Needs of Your Counterpart

In most cases, we are forced to make hard decisions where some people have to lose for others to gain. However, you can develop a mindset of interrogating this win-lose narrative to find a collaborative path. The best way to do this is by striving to understand the needs of the other person and integrating them into your own. This can help you address everyone's underlying need to create solutions that value those needs. Even in situations where the solution doesn't meet every single need, everyone will feel positive about the outcome because some of their needs were met.

Weigh Your Long-term Options

There are times when you may be tempted to be competitive so that you can succeed at another person's expense. Think of two branches of a company competing to attract more clients. If the two have a functional relationship with one another, competing with a win-lose mentality may end up hurting both. The one that wins may savor their victory for a short period but could suffer down the road because the relationship has been sacrificed.

Respect the Other Person

When you are involved in a confrontation, it is easy to fall into the trap of disrespecting the other person in an attempt to win the duel. The problem is that you end up affecting their feelings and attitude toward you. Though you may come out on top this time, your counterpart may not feel comfortable working with you in the future.

If it is a supplier for your business, they may not go out of their way to provide you with the best quality products or services as they used to. What you thought was a win-lose ends up being a lose-lose. If it's a personal relationship, that disrespectful comment or action that shuts the other person down can ultimately ruin the trust between you. By respecting the other person even during a conflict, you can control your emotions long enough to devise a win-win situation.

Be Prepared to Walk Away

Engaging in negotiations can be tough, and it would be naïve to think that you can win every single time. There are times when one party must lose more than the other, and this may mean that you cannot find a workable solution that is mutually beneficial. In such a scenario, the only way to achieve a win-win is for both parties to walk away without a deal. Think of it as agreeing to agreeably disagree. This is usually easier to do before any contracts are established.

Let's say you are hiring an expert to work on one of your specialized projects. The recruit is competent and qualified but during the negotiations, you realize that values and goals aren't aligned. As hard as you try, you simply cannot come to terms. In such a situation, it is best for both parties to agree to disagree and walk away. If nobody is willing to walk away, one party may acquiesce only to later be resentful for what they consider to be an unfair deal.

When you are prepared to walk away, you reduce the pressure to manipulate people to get your way. You are open and transparent, and you genuinely try to understand the other person's position. This allows you to focus single-mindedly on a win-win scenario, and if that fails, you always have the option of walking away.

When you are developing the above skills, you should keep in mind that context is important. Don't conflate influence with manipulation. If you want to become an influential person, you must adopt different approaches for different situations. Effective and ethical leaders know the right time and place to appeal to the head, heart, or hands. You need to understand why you are influencing people and clearly state your goals and values to those involved. This is the best way to ensure authenticity and have the greatest impact on others.

7

SPEAKING WITH IMPACT

One trait that defines a powerful and confident communicator is their ability to speak with impact. An effective communicator can get their message across in a way that connects with the audience and generates a good response. In this chapter, you will discover how to speak with impact and create a message that matters.

Levels of Impact

Few people have developed the art of making an impact using their speech. Most who have done so only developed it after decades of experience in their careers. Yet, this is a skill that every professional must learn because you are always interacting with others and trying to influence those around you. You are at a great disadvantage if you cannot command people's attention and get them to accept your message.

You already know that people have different ways of speaking, and everyone has a different level of impact with their message. However, learning how to speak with impact is a gradual progression from one level to the next. As you move higher up the levels, you improve the impact you have on your audience.

The first level of speaking is attracting people and triggering their interest in your message. Your goal is to ensure that the audience keeps listening to you. In the second level, the goal is to make your message easy to absorb. These first two stages are focused on making your message as compelling as possible. The third level of impact speaking is explaining your message clearly so that the audience can understand it correctly. In the fourth level, your focus is primarily on justifying your ideas to the audience. Once you've grabbed their attention, then you have to persuade them to agree with you. In the fifth level, you focus on using tactics that ensure the audience remembers the key parts of your message. You can use emotional and psychological cues to influence the thoughts and actions of the audience. Finally, at the sixth level, your ideas start to change people's minds, and the audience is ready to do whatever you suggest.

Techniques for Impactful Communication

Making an impact on people is more than just your appearance or the words you use. There are specific techniques that can help make your message more impactful. Though these strategies are simple, you have to keep practicing until you master them. Here are five ways of developing impactful communication:

Keep Your Message Clear and Simple

Have you ever listened to an expert in a particular field talk about a topic, but couldn't seem to grasp what they are trying to say? You look around at the rest of the audience, and everyone seems to have a glazed look in their eyes as if it's a zombie scene from *The Walking Dead*. This is what happens when the person speaking suffers from the "curse of knowledge".

When you are an expert at something, you're so comfortable with the complexities and subtleties of a topic that you often become handicapped at talking about it. You have so many ideas you want to share that you end up mashing them up when speaking to an audience. You have to realize that most people are already overloaded with information. Therefore, to make an impact, you have to focus on one idea at a time and present it clearly and simply.

First, you should talk about your central idea. Explain it using analogies and comparisons, then justify your perspective. You should also try to demonstrate it using a series of steps. Once your audience has grabbed hold of that simplified idea, you can move onto the next one. As you close your message, make sure to summarize your core idea in a few sentences before making recommendations to the audience.

Learn How to Listen

Most people believe that to have an impact on others, you have to be the know-it-all who always has a lot to say. Though there's nothing wrong with having plenty to say, people are more likely to find you interesting if you are a good listener as well. Every great communicator understands the power of listening because it shows others that you think their words are important. This creates trust between the speaker and the audience.

Use Your Body Language

If you want to communicate with impact through body language, focus on three things: posture, poise, and eye contact. We've all been told at one point or another that we should stand up straight. The reason is that it creates a perception of confidence and credibility. For some reason, people tend to pay more attention to taller people. Therefore, if you want to communicate with people, you might as well stand up to your full height. Imagine you're a puppet, and the puppeteer is pulling a string attached to the top of your head. Let your back, shoulders, and neck follow the direction of the string.

Poise refers to how you carry yourself. When speaking to someone, you should stand or sit square to them. This conveys that you are open, transparent and that your message can be trusted. Good poise is based on the angle of your feet. Imagine you're standing up having a face-to-face conversation with someone. Think of an imaginary line that bisects the angle of your feet. Ideally, this line should go *through* the person you're speaking to. If it doesn't, it indicates that you subconsciously want to be somewhere else.

Using eye contact is a subtle art that requires a bit of tact. You don't want to stare into someone's eyes as if you're trying to suck out their soul. Lock eyes with them when you're talking but break contact before they become uncomfortable. It takes a while to learn how to do this well. However, you can practice by making eye contact while listening. Over time, you'll automatically know when it's the right time to break eye contact.

Have a Clear Objective

When it comes to having a clear objective and persuading an audience, one of the most effective tools ever created is the television commercial. The creators of TV commercials have perfected the art of focusing on an objective and achieving its maximum effect. Their goal is to convince the audience that a product or service is the best solution for whatever problem they may have. Well, this is the same thing you're trying to do when communicating with others.

Whether it's an idea, a vision, a product, or a service, you should have a clear objective for the message you want to convey. Think about the thoughts, emotions, and actions you want your message to trigger. Instead of simply passing along information, focus on moving people with the power and sincerity of your words. Let the passion for your purpose shine through as you communicate with the audience.

Use Hooks, Metaphors, and Visual Stimuli

The opening statements of your speech should be so compelling that the audience becomes hooked on everything you say after that. You have to catch people from the very start so that they stick with you until you reveal your core message. If you don't do this, they may have tuned out by the time you reach the essential part of your message.

Metaphors are also another useful tool when trying to make an impact. A metaphor is a figure of speech that suggests a likeness between two things even though they are not the same. Descriptive metaphors evoke feelings and thoughts that capture the mind of the audience: for example, "time is money", "love is a battlefield", or "you're living in a bubble". The images that come to mind can help the audience connect to an abstract truth.

Finally, you can use visual stimuli to make your speech more impactful. Research shows that visual stimuli are the most dynamic aspects of cogent non-verbal communication. They include not just actual images but word-pictures as well. You can use word-pictures in the form of a story to illustrate your point. By using evocative words, a story can paint a picture that captivates an audience's attention throughout your speech.

Importance of Presentation Skills

Communicating with impact is much more than just using the right techniques. The amount of impact you have on others will also depend heavily on your presentation skills. Your ability to present information clearly and effectively plays a major role in whether you get your message across.

But what exactly are presentation skills? It is a set of skills that allows you to interact with your audience, clearly convey your message, engage with them, and understand their mindset. When you have good presentation skills, you can enhance the way you communicate your messages and improve your ability to persuade others.

Emphasis is placed on good presentation skills in the workplace. They are essential in almost every field of expertise, and most people are required to routinely give presentations. While some have a natural knack for picking up good presentation skills, others struggle to do the same. But there's no denying that these skills have a massive influence on your ability to convince clients, customers, colleagues, and senior executives. A manager with good presentation skills is more effective at conveying the vision and mission of the organization to subordinates. Even a low-level employee has to learn how to present ideas to co-workers when they need some kind of assistance.

There are specific benefits that come with good presentation skills. The first is growth and confidence. In today's business world, you may interact with people from around the world. If you speak with greater impact than others, you can attract the attention of influential people who are always on the lookout for new talent. Good presentation skills boost your self-confidence because you can see the positive impact that your message is having on the audience. Furthermore, it adds a flair to your personality that holds the attention of an audience long enough to pass your message.

Secondly, good presentation skills play a key role in understanding your audience. Great speakers know that they have to create a rapport with the audience right from the start. The only way to do this is by studying your target audience and preparing for them in advance. This skill is very useful when you're trying to strike business deals and gain clients. Once you've taken the time to understand the other party's background, you can effectively mold your sales pitch according to their characteristics. The same applies whether you're updating stakeholders at a meeting or teaching a class. You should understand each group's peculiarities and use that information to increase your chances of successfully transmitting your message.

Finally, good presentation skills can make you a great asset to an organization. This is especially true if you're working where seminars and presentations are the norm. Your presentation skills may put you in the limelight and increase your chances of success.

Strategies for Improving Your Presentation Skills

There is a considerable amount of effort that goes into developing good presentation skills. However, it is possible to learn and improve these skills by spending more time practicing them. Here are four ways to enhance your presentation skills:

Proper Preparation

Let's face it. Most people are terrified of speaking in public, especially if it's a large audience. However, it's possible to allay these fears through proper preparation. This is the most important part of a successful presentation. Think of your preparation as the foundation that your whole presentation stands on. If you have strong preparation, you will have an effective presentation. If not, your message will suffer.

Part of your preparation should include researching the audience. This enables you to figure out the best way to reach your target audience based on its unique traits. For example, if you're talking to an analytical audience, such as a group of accountants, you will probably need to show a lot of calculations and graphs in your presentation. This may not work if you're presenting information to an audience of artists and entertainers. The occasion for your presentation also matters. While it may be necessary to provide PowerPoint slides at a trade conference, you would raise eyebrows if you showed up with a projector to make a speech at a wedding. Not all presentations are the same, so be prepared to tailor your approach accordingly.

Another way to prepare is to do a lot of practice. Spend some time rehearsing to identify any flaws and eliminate errors in your message. Do not try to memorize the entire message as this makes it appear mechanical. An audience prefers to watch a presentation that flows freely and is naturally engaging. Adequate practice gives you the confidence to communicate the right message in the best way possible.

Take Charge of the Room

It may be hard to believe, but in general, the audience wants you to succeed. The audience has shown up to listen to you and enjoy the presentation. They want to sit back, give you control of the room and see what you have to say. It is up to you to take charge of the occasion and lead from the front.

One thing to keep in mind is that if you're not connecting with the audience, then you should change your strategy. Have you ever watched a presentation where the presenter has lost the audience but continued to plod through their message for the next 20 minutes? People are busy scrolling through their phones, chatting away, or waiting for a coffee break. As the presenter, you can tell when the audience is tuning out. However, you are not helpless in this case. You can still take charge of the room by adjusting certain things.

You can choose to skip some slides and move to a more interesting section of your presentation. You shouldn't drone on about boring fluff that the audience isn't interested in. Keep in mind that too much text encourages the audience to read from the screen rather than listen to you. If you have too many textual slides, shift over to the ones with images to regain the attention of the audience. You can also use your personality to add a level of engagement to the meeting. For example, if you're a naturally funny person, you can crack some jokes when appropriate to keep the audience tuned in.

The common practice is to wait until the end of a presentation to ask questions. However, this is not a strict rule. You can encourage the audience to ask questions during the presentation. This means that you have to be ready to respond to positive or negative feedback. This may cause you to veer off-script, but at least you'll get the audience to engage in a discussion with you. You are in charge and always have options to ensure that the audience receives your message.

Cope with Your Anxiety

Feeling anxious before giving a presentation is normal. We usually assume that journalists, actors, politicians, teachers, and preachers never feel nervous, but this is not true. Many professionals feel nervous every time they give a presentation despite having years of experience doing it. This means that feeling nervous isn't a weakness to overcome. The queasy stomach, sweaty hands, and dry throat are all part and parcel of presenting in front of an audience. All you have to do is learn how to use that nervous energy to your advantage. Instead of trying to control your nerves, use all that adrenaline to communicate passionately, enthusiastically, and convincingly.

The first step to managing your presentation nerves is to prepare. Take the time to practice your presentation in front of family or a mirror. The more you rehearse, the more confident you become in your ability to successfully deliver the message. If possible, visit the venue, and get familiar with the setup. You should also ensure that everything you will need is available.

Another way to calm your nerves is by staying healthy. You are more likely to feel nervous if your mind and body are unhealthy. You should avoid alcohol and reduce caffeine intake the day before the presentation. If possible, engage in some exercise the day before. A good workout releases endorphins, hormones responsible for pleasure. It also improves your sleep so that you wake up the day of the big event feeling more refreshed. In terms of nutrition, you should eat fruits and vegetables to give you energy.

If you are feeling nervous just as the presentation starts, practice some deep breathing. This will increase the oxygen supply to your brain and put you in a calm state. It will also help prevent your voice from quivering, which is often a side-effect of shallow breathing. You should also drink some water to prevent your mouth from drying, which can cause you to be tongue-tied. Some studies show that chewing gum can help you stay relaxed and boost your alertness. However, don't forget to toss the gum before you begin the presentation. Massaging your forehead also helps you deal with anxiety as it energizes the speech center of the brain.

These techniques are effective for coping with anxiety before the presentation. But what do you do to maintain your relaxed state during the presentation?

The simplest things to do are to pause between sentences, smile, and make eye contact with the audience. The pause gives you time to gather your thoughts, and the body language helps you build rapport with your listeners. You should also slow down your rate of speaking and move around a little to use up any nervous energy.

The most effective way of overcoming nervousness in future presentations is to gather enough experience in the process. After the presentation is over, spend some time collecting feedback from the audience. Listen to any negative feedback but see it as a learning opportunity rather than a failure. Look at the positive aspects of your presentation and reward yourself to celebrate your achievement.

Positive Visualization

This is a technique that enables you to master real-world scenarios and achieve your goals by leveraging the power of positive thinking. Think of it as a mental rehearsal where you visualize a situation as positive before it happens. Studies show that when you are optimistic about life, you feel happier, more confident, and energetic. Others are also more likely to find you sociable and influential.

There are times in life when you may feel low and hopeless. Positive visualization can be a source of inspiration and hope, preventing you from spiraling downward into defeat and depression. By practicing positive visualization, negative thoughts no longer have space in your mind. It also enhances your focus because as you repeatedly visualize the same positive outcome, your brain channels more energy into this mental exercise.

It is important to understand that positive visualization is not a substitute for hard work, practice, and determination. It is simply an effective tool for dealing with self-doubt and low motivation when trying to achieve your goals. So how do you do it?

You should start by visualizing the various steps you will go through before and during your presentation. Try to be as accurate and detailed as possible as you mentally simulate the experience. If you visited the venue and saw the room layout, use these details to strengthen your visualization. Imagine yourself giving your presentation to an enthusiastic audience that is smiling and reacting positively to your message. Feel the positive emotions as strongly as possible so that you burn this experience into your mind. This creates muscle memory that will come in handy during the actual event. Recall the image and its emotions right before you start the presentation.

There are specific tools that can help you during your visualization process. These include:

- **Meditation** – This enables you to focus on your breathing as well as any goals that you need to visualize. You can meditate by yourself or use a guided meditation.
- **Guided Audio Programs** – These can help

guide your thought process during your visualization.

- **Vision Boards** – Create a homemade poster with images and phrases that trigger positive thoughts and emotions related to your presentation. Place these posters in places where you can easily see them.

Visualization helps you develop the clarity of your message and is the most effective way to convey it to the audience.

Capturing the Audience

In today's world, it is a huge struggle to get an audience to focus on your message. There are so many distractions competing for their attention, whether it's their smartphone or a chatty neighbor. If you want to capture the attention of your listeners and maintain that connection, you have to be armed with a bag of tricks. Here are seven tips and tactics you can use:

1. **Create a Plan for Success** – Every great speaker has an outline of their message and masters it so they can communicate it by heart. This is not an easy thing to do. You need to draft and edit your speech multiple times as you rehearse. The more prepared you are, the more comfortable you will be during your presentation.

2. **Give Your Audience What They Want** – Your presentation time is limited so provide your audience with the best value within that timeframe. Start your presentation by offering a quick synopsis of what you are going to be talking about. This way, your audience knows what to expect.

3. **Connect with the Audience on a Personal Level** – Use real stories of real experiences to hook their attention instead of facts and figures that they are likely to forget. The most moving speeches are those where the speaker shares their real experiences to communicate a message and make it more relatable. Don't be afraid of sharing something embarrassing or painful. Anything that relates to your message can be useful in forging a personal bond with the audience. They will become interested in you on a human level rather than seeing you as just another stranger in their midst.

4. **Use Body Language** – Your tone of voice, volume, facial expressions, posture, and eye contact are all sending a message that is as loud as your verbal one. Therefore, you can use the right body language to enhance your presentation. However, if you are not careful, your body language may also ruin your presentation. Avoid actions such as playing with your hair, touching your face, or fidgeting from one foot to the other. These are signs of nervousness and may distract

your audience. Keep your stance open and walk around the podium as much as possible. This projects confidence and keeps the different sections of the audience engaged.

5. **Customize Your Message** – Make it fit the audience's level of knowledge. Never assume that your audience understands the information in the same way that you do. For example, you may want to use jargon when talking to industry insiders. However, some people in the audience may not be as knowledgeable as the rest so avoid too much insider lingo.

6. **Employ Light Humor When Appropriate** – This helps the audience relax and remember the message. However, be careful with the jokes you use. Avoid topics that are polarizing, such as politics or religion. If in doubt, tell the joke to a few friends and gauge their response. It's better to double-check with your peers before you thoroughly embarrass yourself in front of senior company executives.

7. **Pace Yourself** – There is no point in rushing through your message if nobody can hear or understand what you're saying. Slow down and use pauses to allow people to absorb what you've just said. Speakers with a measured tone tend to come across as more capable and knowledgeable than those who talk too quickly.

When it comes to speaking with impact, you need to know how to convey your message clearly and effectively. You want people to remember what you said and how you made them feel. The best way to make an impact is to develop your ability to connect with your audience and hold their attention until they get the message.

CONCLUSION

Learning how to be assertive is one of the most important things you can do in your life. Assertiveness has a huge impact on the way you see yourself, relate to others, and communicate with the world around you. This book has taken you on a journey of discovering what it means to be assertive and how to confidently communicate with power and impact. You have discovered how emotional intelligence influences your social interactions and how a low EQ can be a barrier to effective communication. You now understand the importance of developing a can-do attitude and how to use reframing to cope with negativity. It should be clear to you that self-motivation rather than obligation is the best way to achieve success and inspire others. With the information you've learned here, you are ready to exert more influence in the workplace and handle all your negotiations with a win-win mindset.

Though the book has now come to an end, your journey of self-awareness and empowerment has only just begun. You need to practice the strategies and techniques that have been described in this book. As you do so, you will begin to see positive changes in your personal and professional life. Here are the key takeaways from each chapter:

CHAPTER ONE

- Assertiveness means confidently standing up for yourself and expressing your thoughts and feelings directly without disrespecting the rights of others. It is the balance between aggressive and passive communication.
- The benefits of assertiveness include greater self-awareness and confidence, improved management and negotiating skills, job satisfaction, better problem-solving, and less stress.
- To become more assertive, you have to develop specific skills. You need to improve your self-awareness, set and share clear goals, adopt confident body language, and speak your truth.

Avoid apologizing for your assertiveness and stop being a people-pleaser.
- Self-confidence is not self-esteem. The former is based on your skills or abilities while the latter is based on how you evaluate your worth as an individual.
- Self-confidence is important because it makes you bolder, more motivated and lowers your stress levels. It also increases your sense of self, improves your resilience, and boosts your social influence and leadership potential. Your sexual attractiveness is also enhanced and you end up with more fulfilling relationships.
- To boost your self-confidence, you should practice positive self-talk, visualization, and increased risk-taking. You should also understand your strengths and weaknesses, enhance your skills, change your body image, associate with positive people, and improve your posture.

CHAPTER TWO

- Emotional intelligence is defined by four attributes: self-management, self-awareness, social awareness, and relationship management.
- It is important to understand emotional

intelligence because it affects your performance and social interactions. It impacts your communication, helps you manage your emotions, and enables you to empathize with others. It also influences your physical, emotional, and mental health.
- Individuals who have high emotional intelligence display several important signs. They reflect on their feelings, properly manage their thoughts, accept criticism, and stay true to their values. They also give constructive feedback, let go of the past, are comfortable apologizing, protect themselves from emotional manipulation, and show empathy.
- Emotional intelligence is measured using an emotional quotient (EQ), which is a score you attain on a standardized test. EQ can be measured using performance tests such as MSCEIT (*Mayer-Salovey-Caruso Emotional Intelligence Test*) or ESCI (*Emotional and Social Competency Inventory*). You can also use self-reporting tests such as the Emotional Quotient Inventory (EQ-i).
- Whereas emotional intelligence is based on cognitive ability, emotional competence is based on your performance and how you express feelings during social interactions.

- There are three steps to communicating your emotions effectively. First, identify your emotions, then interpret and perceive them, and finally find healthy ways to express negative emotions through art, music, etc.

CHAPTER THREE

- Communication is the sending and receiving of information to achieve understanding. This is done either verbally or non-verbally.
- Communication skills are important because they affect how you establish relationships and interact with others. How you communicate also reveals your knowledge and sincerity to others.
- Being an effective communicator has many benefits. It boosts your chances of being hired on your terms during an interview, shows your leadership skills, and helps defuse conflict. It also enlarges your social network and makes you a better learner.
- Some of the barriers to effective communication include stress, lack of focus, and inconsistent body language.
- To develop good communication skills, you must become a good listener, learn to read non-

verbal cues, and ask open-ended questions during conversations. You should also become more assertive and find ways to manage your stress levels.
- An effective communicator always tries to understand the audience. This is achieved by acquiring more information about the audience, using powerful language when speaking to them, acknowledging their diverse tastes, and customizing your message to suit those preferences.

CHAPTER FOUR

- A can-do attitude is a mental attitude of confidence in your ability to achieve goals and create the life you want.
- It shifts your mindset away from weakness and victimhood to one of strength and success. It also changes the way you view and interact with the world around you.
- To develop a can-do mindset, you need to adopt a growth and learning mindset. You have to find accountability partners to keep you focused and avoid excessive self-criticism. You also need to align your thoughts, emotions, and actions before acting on your ideas. Don't

forget to incorporate fun activities in your life as well!
- Showing enthusiasm when speaking attracts your audience and shows them that you are well-prepared and informed. It also shows that you are invested in your speech.
- To communicate enthusiasm, use active speech and power language to grab people's attention. It also helps to love the topic of discussion. When communicating via writing, separate the text using subsections and use bullet points.
- Reframing is a cognitive coping strategy used when dealing with a negative situation. It enables you to change your perspective about a difficult situation from negative to positive.
- Reframing helps manage stress, promote innovation, generate creative solutions, and make better decisions.
- There are several strategies for reframing. You can rethink the question, consider so-called bad ideas, and even challenge some of your assumptions. You can also break the problem down into smaller ones and seek advice from a wide range of people.

CHAPTER FIVE

- Self-motivation is an inner force that drives you to work toward your goals so that you can grow and achieve personal fulfillment.
- It helps you cope better with stress, leads to greater satisfaction, and can be an inspiration to others.
- To develop self-motivation, you need to know your values and your *why* (your reason for doing that particular task). You should also reframe your language, surround yourself with motivated people, and become a continuous learner.
- You can also be motivated by listening to music, reading a motivational book, or watching an inspiring movie. There are also guided meditations, affirmations, and visualizations you can use to generate self-motivation.
- The best way to inspire others is to appeal to their emotions. You need to identify their unique motivators and set clear goals that challenge them. In the workplace, you should establish a motivating environment that brings out the best in them.

CHAPTER SIX

- Influence is the ability to produce the desired outcome without getting attached to the result. Control, on the other hand, is seeking to guarantee the desired outcome by any means necessary.
- You can exert influence over others in three ways: through logical appeal (sharing the rationale behind your idea), emotional appeal (connecting to their values), and cooperative appeal (consultation and teamwork).
- Influencing others should come from a place of authenticity, i.e., staying true to your values and walking the talk.
- Some of the strategies for exerting influence in the workplace include developing organizational intelligence, tactical self-promotion, and building trust. You also gain influence by respecting people's opinions, becoming an expert in your field, and watching your body language.
- Negotiating is a measure of your influence. Your negotiation skills determine how well you present yourself and your ideas and whether you can convince people to help you reach your goals.

- To become a master negotiator, you need to have confidence, prepare well, and study the other person's motivations. You have to become an active listener who can control your emotions. You should also be flexible with your strategy and be willing to make concessions.
- You need to develop a win-win mindset to achieve a positive outcome for all parties involved in a negotiation. This is possible by having an abundance mindset and being considerate of the other person's needs. You should also think long-term and be willing to walk away if no agreement can be made.

CHAPTER SEVEN

- Powerful and confident communicators have mastered how to speak with impact. They understand and apply the different levels of speaking to get their message across to the audience.
- There are five techniques for impactful speaking: keeping the message simple, listening well, using body language, having a clear objective, and using visual stimuli.
- Presentation skills are a set of skills that allow you to interact with your audience, clearly

convey your message, engage with them, and understand their mindset.

- Good presentation skills give you confidence when speaking and help you understand your audience. They also expose you to numerous growth opportunities, thus making you invaluable to an organization.
- To improve your presentation skills, you need proper preparation before you step onto the podium. Positive visualization tools such as meditation or vision boards are handy when preparing. You must also learn how to take charge of the room and cope with anxiety during the presentation.
- To capture the audience's attention, create a plan of how you will give them information that they value. When communicating, connect with their emotions by using the right body language, customizing your message, and adding humor when appropriate. You should also pace your speech to make sure your message is received clearly.

I am grateful and honored that you have taken the time to dive into this book. The information can take you a long way if you implement the strategies and techniques provided here. You can improve your relationships by learning how to communicate confidently and effectively. You can set your career prospects on an upward trajectory by being more assertive. Avoid passive and aggressive communication styles as these may gradually ruin your relationships and limit your ability to succeed in the long term.

This book has shown you how you can improve your communication and leadership skills both at home and in the workplace. Now that you have the tools you need, you are well-equipped to go and use them to make the changes you need. Your life will never be the same again!

PRAISE FOR MARLENE GONZALEZ

Dear Reader,

I hope you like it!

As a self-publishing author, I rely on readers like you to help promote my work and serve humanity better by doing my best to write, share, coach and train the next generation of leaders like you.

Please, consider posting an online review on Amazon, a short review, audio, or a picture highlighting the page you enjoyed the most. Book reviews are essential to any book. They help potential buyers make confident decisions when getting and buying books.

www.amazon.com/review/create-review/asin=B099KNLYL1/

Unlock the leader in you.

Your coach, Marlene Gonzalez.

ABOUT THE AUTHOR

Marlene Gonzalez is the founder and the president of Life coaching group LLC. focusing on Leadership development and executive coaching. She passionately pursues one vision- "To advance, develop and promote minority leaders." She is a renowned executive  coach and facilitator. She is the author of the coaching series Leadership Wizard; "Number 1 New Release book in the Education and Leadership category". Her book series specializes in transformational leadership topics such as:

- *Leadership Wizard. The Nine Dimensions. Unlock the Leader in You. The Discipline of Coaching Yourself to Fearlessly Lead, Influence, Inspire and Empower Others.*

- *Assertive Wizard. How To Boost Confidence, Get Your Message Across, And Speak With Impact.*
- *Change Wizard. Master The Art Of Leading Change And Working Together for a Common Purpose.*
- *Confident Wizard.* Turn Self Doubt Into Confidence: The Ultimate Guide To Lead With Authenticity, Purpose, and Resilience.

Once you master these and many other topics she covers, you can transform your life and become a more successful leader. In addition, you will find that her books have a straight-to-the-point approach and easy to implement actions. She is passionate about sharing her insights and resources on transformational leadership through a combination of Insights Discovery, the psychology of C. G. Jung, her corporate career experience and her professional coaching expertise.

González held many executive corporate positions in the US, Europe, and Latin America. She is the former Senior Director of Global Training, Learning, and Development for McDonald's Corporation. Marlene holds a BS, an Executive MBA/PAG, and a graduate diploma on managerial Issues in the global enterprise from Thunderbird University. www.marlenegonzalez.com

ALSO BY MARLENE GONZALEZ

AVAILABLE ON AUDIBLE

THE SELF COACHING GUIDE TO MASTER THE ART OF LEADERSHIP AND CHANGE LIKE A PRO

Two in One Bundle

Leadership comes from within, but you can't find it until you know where to look. Here's what you need to know…The power is within you and become a true wizard!

Sign up Now to get free resources and more!

www.marlenegonzalez.com

REFERENCES

Asman, Z. (2018, March 1). *How important is enthusiasm when communicating?* Medium. https://medium.com/@zrasman/how-important-is-enthusiasm-when-communicating-91f99bcc5d80

Barriso, J. (2018, Feb 28). *13 signs of high emotional intelligence: Wonder what emotional intelligence looks like in everyday life? Here are 13 examples.* https://www.inc.com/justin-bariso/13-things-emotionally-intelligent-people-do.html

Bennet, T. (2019, March 19). *Being assertive vs. being aggressive: Assertive behavior demonstrates respect and leads to better outcomes than aggression.* Thriveworks. https://thriveworks.com/blog/assertive-vs-aggressive-whats-the-difference/

Bokhari, D. (2020, Nov 26). *How to Develop a Can Do Attitude and Succeed in Life.* Lifehack. https://www.lifehack.org/833809/Can-do-attitude

Centre for Creative Leadership. *Master the 3 ways to influence people.* https://www.ccl.org/articles/leading-effectively-articles/three-ways-to-influence-people/

Cherry, K. (2020, June 3). *What is emotional intelligence?* Verywellmind. https://www.verywellmind.com/what-is-emotional-intelligence-2795423

Clore, G.L. & Zadra, J.R. (2011). *Emotion and perception: The role of affective information.* https://www.ncbi.nlm.nih.gov/pmc/articles/PMC3203022/

Communication Assessment & Learning Lab. (2014, April 22). *How does communication play into our daily lives?* http://comm.lab.asu.edu/how-does-communication-plays-into-our-daily-lives/#.YEj5A9z-hPY

Hayashi, A., Karasawa, M., & Tobin, J. (2009). The Japanese preschool's pedagogy of feeling: Cultural strategies for supporting young children's emotional development. *Ethos,* 37(1), 32–49.

Kapur, R. (2020, Sep). *The models of communication.* ResearchGate. https://www.researchgate.net/publication/344295651_The_Models_of_Communication

Mackler, C. *5 easy ways to communicate better in your relationship.* OneLove. https://www.joinonelove.org/learn/5-easy-ways-to-communicate-better-in-your-relationships/

Mayo Clinic. (2020, May 29). *Being assertive: Reduce stress, communicate better.* https://www.mayoclinic.org/healthy-lifestyle/stress-management/in-depth/assertive/art-20044644

McNamara, C. *Reframing for problem solving (To see things differently).* Free Management Library. https://managementhelp.org/personalproductivity/reframing.htm

Meier, J.D. (2016, March 18). *15 ways to motivate yourself and others.* Time. https://time.com/4262774/motivation-ways/

Mwaka, C.W.L. *Benefits of win-win mindset.* The Wise Entrepreneur. https://www.thewiseentrepreneur.co.ug/tag/benefits-of-win-win-mindset/

O'Hara, C. (2014, June 6). *How to negotiate with someone more powerful than you.* Harvard Business Review. https://hbr.org/2014/06/how-to-negotiate-with-someone-more-powerful-than-you

Opre, A. & Vaida, S. (2014). Emotional intelligence versus emotional competence. *Journal of Psychological and Educational Research.* https://www.marianjournals.com/files/JPER_articles/JPER_22_1_2014/Vaida_Opre_JPER_2014_22_1_26_33.pdf

Pattnaik, C. (2020, July 18). *Everything you need to know about positive visualization, the ultimate technique to help you achieve your goals.* Healthshots. https://www.healthshots.com/mind/happiness-hacks/everything-you-need-to-know-about-positive-visualization/

Ravenscraft, E. (2019, June 3). *Practical ways to improve your confidence (and why you should).* The New York Times. https://www.inc.com/justin-bariso/13-things-emotionally-intelligent-people-do.html

Robbins, T. *8 ways to improve communication and find more fulfillment.* https://www.tonyrobbins.com/ultimate-relationship-guide/key-communication-relationships/#

Seal, C.R. & Andrews-Brown, A. (2010). An integrative model of emotional intelligence: Emotional ability as a moderator of the mediated relationship of emotional quotient and emotional competence. *Organization Management Journal,* 7, 143–152. doi: 10.1057/omj.2010.22

Schuneman, F. (2020, April 28). *7 key-steps to motivate and inspire your team.* Invista. https://www.

invistaperforms.org/7-key-steps-to-motivate-and-inspire-your-team/

Schwantes, M. (2017, Nov 30). *8 things the smartest leaders do to motivate their employees.* Inc. https://www.inc.com/marcel-schwantes/8-powerful-ways-to-motivate-inspire-your-employees-this-week.html

Stone, D. (2012, October 24). *Emotional intelligence and emotional competence.* Psychological Musings. https://psychological-musings.blogspot.com/2012/10/emotional-intelligence-and-emotional.html

The Blog. (2018, September 12). *Assertiveness Vs Aggression: Characteristics of When Assertiveness Become Aggression.* https://www.allos.com.au/communication-skills/assertiveness-vs-aggression-characteristics-assertiveness-become-aggression/

Tow, H. (2020, Feb 3). *9 tips for improving your presentation skills for your next meeting.* Venggage. https://venngage.com/blog/presentation-skills/

www.ingramcontent.com/pod-product-compliance
Lightning Source LLC
Chambersburg PA
CBHW030112240426
43673CB00002B/47